WINDOWS WITH EASE

CREATIVE PUBLISHING international

CHANHASSEN, MINNESOTA
www.creativepub.com

D1122859

WINDOWS
WITH EASE

Copyright © 2003
Creative Publishing international, Inc.
18705 Lake Drive East
Chanhassen, Minnesota 55317
1-800-328-3895
www.creativepub.com
All rights reserved

President/CEO: Michael Eleftheriou
Vice President/Publisher: Linda Ball
Vice President/Retail Sales: Kevin Haas

WINDOWS WITH EASE
Created by the editors of Creative Publishing international, Inc.

Executive Editor: Alison Brown Cerier
Managing Editor: Yen Le
Senior Editor: Linda Neubauer
Art Director & Illustrator: Megan Noller
Cover Design: Michaelis Carpelis Design
Project & Photo Stylist: Joanne Wawra
Samplemakers: Arlene Dohrman, Teresa Henn
Photographer: Tate Carlson
Director of Production Services: Kim Gerber
Production Manager: Stasia Dorn
Contributors: Colorful Quilts & Textiles (www.colorfulquilts.com);
Nancy Eato; Elaine Perry; Te-MA (www.te-ma.com); Umbra Inc.
(www.umbra.com); Wrights (www.wrights.com)

ISBN 1-58923-070-1

Printed on American paper by:
  R. R. Donnelley
10 9 8 7 6 5 4 3 2 1

Library of Congress Cataloging-in-Publication Data

Windows with ease.
    p. cm.
  Includes index.
  ISBN 1-58923-070-1 (soft cover)
    1. Draperies. 2. Windows in interior decoration. 3. Window shades.
  I. Creative Publishing International.

  TT390.W5525 2003
  746.9′4--dc21

                            2002041764

Creative Publishing international, Inc. offers a variety of
how-to-books. For information write:
    Creative Publishing international, Inc.
        Subscriber Books
    18705 Lake Drive East
    Chanhassen, MN 55317

contents

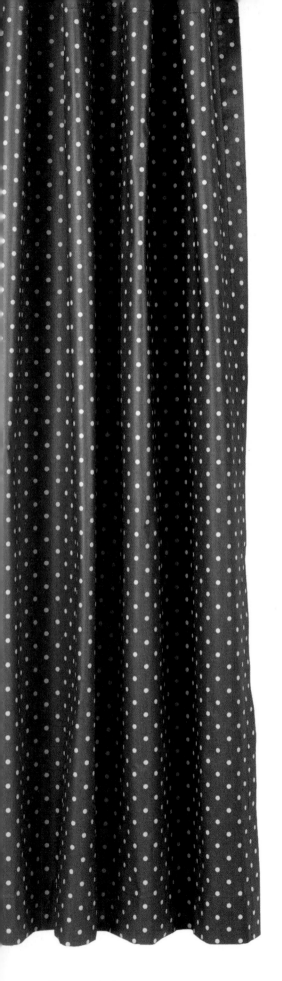

introduction

WINDOWS WITH EASE sounds like a contradiction, doesn't it? After all, making window treatments is a time-consuming, tedious task undertaken only by serious sewers and people who have a genuine flair for decorating. Not anymore! Anyone, regardless of skill level or natural decorating knack, can create a window treatment using the ideas and methods presented in this book.

There are lots of styles to choose from because you will undoubtedly use a variety of window treatment styles throughout your home. Some rooms are more formal than others, where full-length curtains and graceful swags are a fitting complement to your décor. In rooms intended for relaxation and recreation, low-profile window treatments such as tent flap, Roman, or roller shades offer the light control and privacy you need while blending perfectly into the casual atmosphere. Unique top treatments, used alone or layered over more functional treatments, give windows personalities that can become the foundations for distinctive decorating schemes.

Each window treatment style can be created entirely from scratch, if you are a confident sewer. Complete instructions lead you step-by-step through the construction process. All the window designs are simple styles that can be sewn in a day or less. If you can sew but it's not really your cup of tea, shortcuts like fusing hems

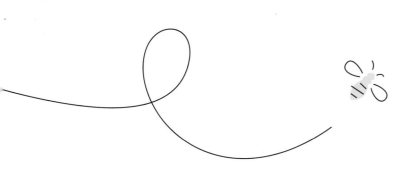

and using self-styling pleater tapes that give you professional results in a shorter time with fewer skill requirements. Even if sewing is out of the question, you can create window treatments with ready-made items such as tablecloths and sheets, or you can add personal embellishments to ready-made curtain panels. Some unique board-mounted toppers require only a glue gun and a little imagination!

Details distinguish your window treatments from the ordinary. With a little creativity, even catalog curtains can be custom-designed to perk up their surroundings. Easy paint techniques, fusible appliqués and banding, or glue-on decorator trims change a ho-hum panel into an expressive room brightener in a matter of minutes. Common hardware-store items such as PVC pipe, coat hooks, and peg rail become useful and decorative elements of a window treatment with a little ingenuity. You'll find lots of examples on pages 102 to 123 to get you thinking.

Whether you spend a weekend or an hour making your window treatment, you want it to be attractive, functional, and durable. You want to be able to say with pride, "I made it myself!" Professional guidelines on pages 126 to 142 help you make and install your treatments quickly and correctly. You'll soon discover that first-rate window treatments truly can be made with ease.

curtains

flat-panel curtains

THIS TRULY VERSATILE curtain style is the foundation for many looks, some rather tailored and contemporary and others very relaxed and luxurious. The basic method for making the curtain panels is the same for all styles and requires only a few simple steps. Three pivotal choices will determine the ultimate style and appearance of these curtains: the fabric selection, the fullness and length desired, and the method of hanging the curtain.

Select firmly woven mediumweight fabric to create a simple tailored look, with an upper edge that can be styled into gentle rolling folds. Lightweight, slinky fabric will result in a relaxed, soft look, with an upper edge that dips gracefully between attachment points. Depending on the desired fullness (two-and-one-half times to one-and-one-half times fullness), one full width of decorator fabric will cover an area 18" to 32" (46 to 81.5 cm) wide. If more width is desired, seam together full or half widths of fabric for each panel (page 138).

As with most curtain styles, sill-length is casual, simpler; floor-length is formal. Spilling-onto-the-floor length is luxurious and opulent and, by necessity, stationary. The panels can be hung from a decorative rod by means of clip-on or sew-on curtain rings that are available in many styles. Grommets can be inserted into the upper hemmed edge for installing with decorative hooks, cording, or ribbon or for being run through directly by a decorative rod or steel cable.

Determine the method for hanging the curtain and mount the hardware (page 129) before you begin so you can accurately measure for the finished length. It is a good idea to mock up a small sample to determine the exact location of the curtain top in relation to the rod; the type of hook or lacing method used greatly affects the measurement.

HOW TO MAKE A BASIC *flat-panel curtain*

MATERIALS

- Decorator fabric, amount determined in step 1

- Carpenter's square

- Thread

- Iron and pressing surface

- Drapery weights for floor-length curtains

- Grommets, hooks, clip-on or sew-on rings, or other means of attachment as desired

- Decorative curtain rod, tension wire, or decorative hooks as desired

1. Measure (page 126) for the finished length of the curtain; add the total bottom hem allowance (chart) and upper hem allowance to find the cut length of each panel. Multiply the cut length by the number of fabric widths needed to determine the amount to buy.

2. Preshrink the fabric (page 136) if you intend to launder the curtains occasionally. Mark the cut lengths along the selvage, and cut the pieces, using a carpenter's square to ensure straight cuts. Trim away the selvages unless you are working with a loosely woven or sheer fabric.

3. Seam fabric widths and half-widths together as necessary. Press under and stitch the lower double-fold hem (page 141). Press under and stitch 1¹/2" (3.8 cm) double-fold side hems, encasing a drapery weight (page 115) in the hem layers at the lower corners of floor-length curtains.

4. Press under a double-fold hem in the upper edge. Unfold the fabric at the upper corners. Trim out the excess fabric from the inner layer, as shown, trimming to within ³/8" (1 cm) of the fold. Refold and stitch the upper hem.

5. Clip-on or sew-on rings: Mark placement along the top hem, placing the end marks ³/4" (2 cm) from the sides. Space the remaining marks evenly 6" to 10" (15 to 25.5 cm) apart. Try different spacing patterns, using safety pins, to help you decide. Attach a ring at each mark.

6. Grommets or buttonholes: Mark the placement for the grommets or buttonholes as for the rings, above. Use an even number of marks if the curtain will be run through by a steel cable or thin rod, so that both ends of the panel will turn inward. Insert the grommets, following the manufacturer's directions.

4

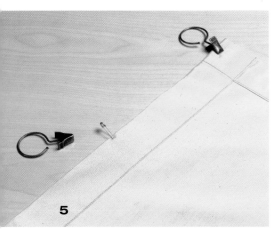

5

6

HEM DEPTHS

CURTAIN LENGTH	BOTTOM HEM ALLOWANCE
To sill or apron	6" (15 cm)
1/2" (1.3 cm) above floor	8" (20.5 cm)
Brushing floor	8" (20.5 cm)
Puddling on floor	1" (2.5 cm)

METHOD OF HANGING	UPPER HEM ALLOWANCE
Clip-on or sew-on rings	3" (7.5 cm)
Grommet or buttonhole	Two times grommet or buttonhole length plus 2" (5 cm)

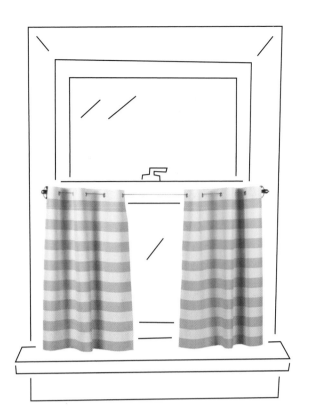

more ideas

LEFT: Short, grommeted curtains over a window seat are mounted on a steel cable. These are no-sew, quick and easy, because the fabric is 32" (81.5 cm) outdoor canvas turned sideways. The neat selvages do not require hemming, and the cut ends don't ravel.

BELOW: Dramatic fringe brushes the floor in these stationary side panels that are ingeniously tied to decorative drawer knobs. Also a no-sew project, these curtains are made from 80" (203.5 cm) fashion shawls.

LEFT: Twin-size bed sheets with decorative hems make lovely curtains, and require no sewing at all. At evenly spaced intervals across the curtain top, fabric is tied into bundles with ribbons and secured to clip-on rings on a decorative rod. Fold excess fabric to the back and experiment to determine the right length.

ABOVE: A purchased linen tablecloth takes on new life as a banded curtain. Coordinating plaid fabric bands were fused (page 111) along the hemmed sides of the tablecloth to complete this easy no-sew treatment.

relaxed rod-pocket curtains

CONTEMPORARY ROD-POCKET curtains are designed to be hung from narrow decorator rods. Unlike their frilly ancestors, these curtains have no heading ruffling above the rod, they are made with less fullness, and the pockets are deep and loose instead of snug-fitting. The result is a more casual, carefree appearance that can be dressed up or down through the choice of fabric. Because rod-pocket styles are necessarily stationary, they may be designed as separate panels hung at the sides of a window or as abutting panels that are parted and pulled back to the sides. One continuous panel may cover the window or be drawn to one side or the center. For a luxurious look, the curtains may be cut with extra length so that the hem brushes or puddles on the floor. A single width of decorator fabric, gathered onto a rod at one-and-one-half to two times fullness will cover 32" to 24" (81.5 to 61 cm). To determine the number of fabric widths needed for wider coverage, multiply the desired finished width by the desired fullness, divide by the fabric width, and round up or down to the nearest whole number.

HOW TO MAKE A *rod-pocket curtain*

MATERIALS

- Decorator fabric, amount determined in step 1
- Carpenter's square
- Thread
- Iron and pressing surface
- Drapery weights for floor-length curtains
- Narrow decorative curtain rod

1. Measure (page 126) for the finished length of the curtain; add the total bottom hem allowance (chart) plus the rod-pocket allowance to find the cut length of each panel. Multiply the cut length by the number of fabric widths needed to determine the amount to buy.

2. Preshrink the fabric (page 136) if you intend to launder the finished curtains occasionally. Mark the cut lengths along the selvage, and cut the pieces, using a carpenter's square to ensure straight cuts. Trim away the selvages unless you are working with a loosely woven or sheer fabric.

3. Seam fabric widths and half-widths together as necessary. Press under and stitch the lower double-fold hem (page 141). Press under and stitch 1¹/2" (3.8 cm) double-fold side hems, encasing a drapery weight (page 115) in the hem layers at the lower corners of floor-length curtains.

4. Press under ¹/2" (1.3 cm) at the upper edge. Then fold under the remaining rod-pocket allowance and pin; do not press a crease into the upper fold. Stitch close to the lower fold, forming the rod pocket.

5. Insert the rod through the pocket and mount the curtain. Distribute fullness evenly along the rod. Style the curtains as desired.

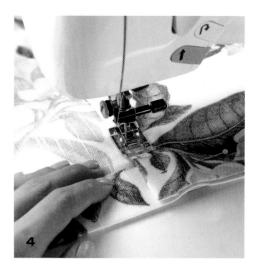

HEM DEPTHS

CURTAIN LENGTH	TOTAL HEM ALLOWANCE	ROD-POCKET ALLOWANCE
To sill or apron	6" (15 cm)	3¹/2" (9 cm)
¹/2" (1.3 cm) above floor	8" (20.5 cm)	5¹/2" (14 cm)
Brushing floor	8" (20.5 cm)	5¹/2" (14 cm)
Puddling on floor	1" (2.5 cm)	5¹/2" (14 cm)

more ideas

LEFT: Cut a chenille bedspread in half and hem the long cut edges. Stitch rod pockets into the upper edges and hang the curtain set with the fringed edges down the center and along the bottom.

BELOW: Layer two sets of coordinating rod-pocket curtains to create this interesting treatment. Hang the back panels on rods. Then run decorative cording through the rod pockets of the front panels, and tie the ends to the rods. Use chair ties to gather up the centers of the front panels and accent the rod ends.

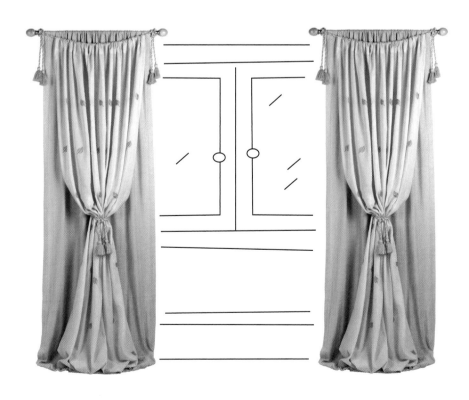

classic rod-pocket curtains

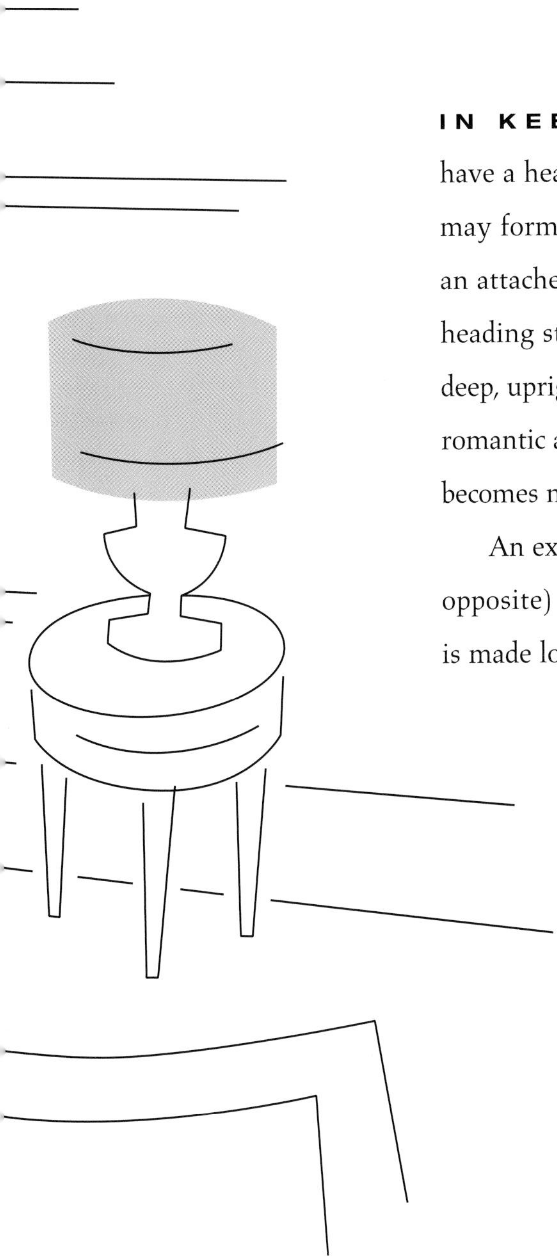

IN KEEPING WITH classic rod-pocket styles, these curtains have a heading above the rod pocket that, depending on its depth, may form a ruffle above the rod or fall forward over the rod forming an attached valance. The rod pocket fits the rod snugly to keep the heading standing upright. With two-and-one-half times fullness and a deep, upright heading, classic rod-pocket curtains take on a feminine, romantic appearance. With less fullness and a shorter heading, the look becomes more tailored and modern.

An extra long heading that forms a soft attached valance (shown opposite) gives the curtain a formal look, especially when the curtain is made long enough to break or puddle on the floor.

MATERIALS

- Decorator fabric, amount determined in step 1

- Carpenter's square

- Thread

- Iron and pressing surface

- Drapery weights for floor-length curtains

- Decorative curtain rod if part of the rod will show or nondecorative rod if it will be completely covered

1. Measure (page 126) for the finished length of the curtain; add the total bottom hem allowance (chart, page 18). To determine the extra length needed for the rod pocket, measure the circumference of the rod and add 1" (2.5 cm). Add twice the desired heading depth to find the cut length of each panel. Multiply the cut length by the number of fabric widths needed to determine the amount to buy.

2. Preshrink (page 136) the fabric if you intend to launder the finished curtains occasionally. Mark the cut lengths along the selvage, and cut the pieces, using a carpenter's square to ensure straight cuts. Trim away the selvages unless you are working with a loosely woven or sheer fabric.

3. Seam fabric widths and half-widths together (page 138) as necessary. Press under and stitch the lower double-fold hem (page 141). Press under and stitch 1½" (3.8 cm) double-fold side hems, encasing a drapery weight in the hem layers at the lower corners of floor-length curtains.

4. Press under ½" (1.3 cm) at the upper edge. Then fold under half the total allowance for the rod pocket and heading; press. Stitch along the bottom fold. Then stitch again a distance from the upper edge equal to the desired depth of the heading.

5. Insert the rod through the pocket and mount the curtain. Distribute fullness evenly along the rod. Style the curtains as desired.

4

more ideas

LEFT: A matelassé bedspread was transformed into a cozy cottage curtain. Stitches holding the upper hem were removed and resewn to make a rod pocket with a deep heading that has been "popped" open.

ABOVE: Plain rod-pocket cafe-curtains purchased from a mail-order catalogue were dressed up by fusing ball fringe above the lower hems.

tab curtains

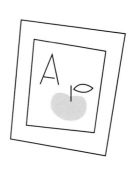

CURTAINS WITH SELF-FABRIC tabs, though simple in style, can require time-consuming sewing. However, there are some shortcut techniques that can speed up the process. The method that follows requires the least amount of fabric while allowing you to use the full width of your fabric for the curtain panel. Each fabric width has five or six evenly spaced tabs; each tab, when folded over a rod, is 5¹/2" (14 cm) long and 1¹/2" (3.8 cm) wide. It is wise to mock up the treatment and hang the rod before cutting for accurate length measurements.

HOW TO MAKE A *tab curtain*

MATERIALS

- Decorator fabric, amount determined in step 1

- Carpenter's square

- Rotary cutter, mat, and quilting ruler helpful for cutting tab strips

- Thread

- Iron and pressing surface

- Paper-backed fusible adhesive, 3/4" (2 cm) wide

- Drapery weights for floor-length curtains

- Decorative curtain rod

1. Measure (page 126) for the finished length of the curtain; add the total bottom hem allowance (chart, page 13) and 3" (7.5 cm) upper hem allowance to find the cut length of each panel. Multiply the cut length by the number of fabric widths needed to determine the total amount required for the curtains. For the tabs, add 12" (30.5 cm) for every two fabric widths needed to determine the total length to buy.

2. Preshrink the fabric (page 136), if you intend to launder the finished curtains occasionally. Mark the cut lengths for the curtains along the selvage, and cut the pieces, using a carpenter's square to ensure straight cuts. Trim away the selvages unless you are working with a loosely woven or sheer fabric.

3. Cut a full-width 12" (30.5 cm) strip for the tabs. Cut it into 3" (7.5 cm) strips on the lengthwise grain, using a rotary cutter, mat, and quilting ruler, if available.

4. Fuse a strip of paper-backed fusible adhesive down the center of each strip, following the manufacturer's directions. Remove the paper backing. Fold the edges into the center and fuse in place.

5. Seam fabric widths and half widths together (page 138) as necessary for each curtain panel. Press under and stitch the lower double-fold hem (page 141).

6. Press under 1/2" (1.3 cm) on the upper edge. Then press 2" (5 cm) to the right side, forming a facing. At the outer corners, stitch the facing to the curtain 3" (7.5 cm) from the edges (arrow). Trim the facing to within 1/4" (6 mm) of the stitching; trim off the top 1" (2.5 cm) of the side hem allowance.

7. Mark the placement for the tabs, evenly spaced along the upper hem of the curtain, with the first and last tabs even with the outer edges. Fold the tabs in half and slide them under the facing with the raw edges in the fold; pin. Stitch across the curtain top, 1/2" (1.3 cm) from the fold.

8. Press under 1 1/2" (3.8 cm) double-fold side hems. Turn the facing to the curtain back; press. Stitch the side hems, encasing a drapery weight (page 115) in the hem layers at the lower corners of floor-length curtains. At upper corners, the hem will disappear under the facing. Stitch along the lower fold of the facing.

3

4

6

7

more ideas

LEFT: Cotton cording tabs are strung through grommets and looped over shelf pegs holding this relaxed seafaring curtain in place. Cotton denim, selvages intact, is cut to length and then laundered to allow the edges to fray.

BELOW: Narrow grosgrain ribbon fused down the center of wider ribbon in a contrasting color make up the tabs for this curtain. The curtain itself is a flat sheet, turned with the decorative hem at the bottom. The tabs are sewn into the top facing; the sheet selvages are used instead of side hems.

ABOVE: Decorator burlap becomes a quick and easy curtain. Simply cut to size, allowing for a short cuff at the top, and fringe the edges. Thread lengths of twine through both layers at evenly spaced intervals for tabs. Tie the tabs to a sturdy branch.

RIGHT: Dress up a plain purchased tab curtain by tying bright ribbons around the base of each tab. Fuse bands of wider ribbons at the hem.

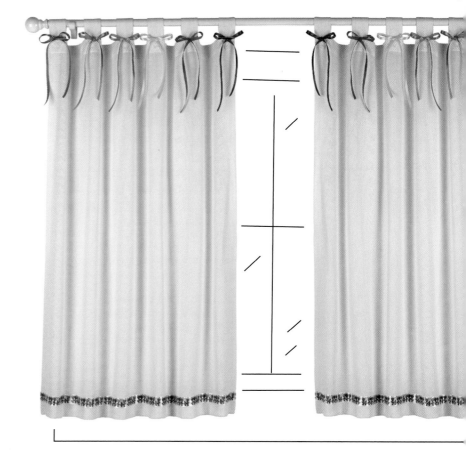

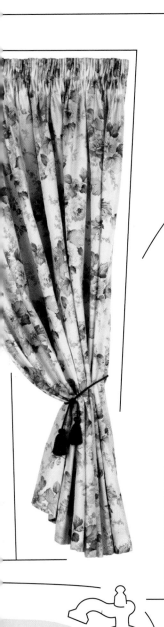

styling tape curtains

WONDERFUL INNOVATIONS OF the sewing industry, styling tapes help even beginning sewers create curtains with intricate headings. The tapes have woven-in cords that, when pulled, draw the fabric fullness into pleats, gathers, or distinctive folds. Most tapes require a flat curtain panel two-and-one-half times the desired finished width, depending on the fabric weight. Information specific to each tape is included inside the package of precut lengths. If you have the tape cut from a large roll, the store should supply you with a brochure.

HOW TO MAKE A *curtain with a styling tape heading*

MATERIALS

- Fabric, amount determined in step 1
- Carpenter's square
- Iron and pressing surface
- Styling tape
- Thread
- Drapery weights for floor-length curtains
- Decorative curtain rod and rings or utility rod and hooks

1. Measure (page 126) for the finished length of the curtain; add the total bottom hem allowance (chart, page 13) plus 1" (2.5 cm) to find the cut length of each panel. Multiply the desired finished width of the curtain by the fullness required for the styling tape; add 6" (15 cm) for side hems, to determine the cut width. Divide the cut width by the fabric width to determine the number of fabric widths required. Multiply the cut length by the number of widths required to determine the amount to buy.

2. Preshrink the fabric (page 136), if you intend to launder the finished curtains occasionally. Mark the cut lengths along the selvage, and cut the pieces using a carpenter's square to ensure straight cuts. Trim away the selvages unless you are working with a loosely woven or sheer fabric.

3. Seam fabric widths together as necessary. Press under and stitch the lower double-fold hem (page 141), encasing a drapery weight at the base of each seam. Press under and stitch 1½" (3.8 cm) double-fold side hems, encasing a drapery weight (page 115) in the hem layers at the lower corners of floor-length curtains.

4. Seam fabric widths together as necessary. Press under 1" (2.5 cm) along the upper edge of the curtain panel. Cut styling tape 3" (7.5 cm) longer than the curtain panel width. Press under 1½" (3.8 cm) on the ends of the tape. Using a pin, pick out cords from the pressed-under ends.

5. Pin the tape, right side up, to the curtain panel, with the upper edge of the tape ½" (1.3 cm) from the upper fold of the curtain. Stitch the tape to the curtain, stitching just inside the top and bottom edges and next to any additional cords. Be careful not to catch the cords in the stitching. Check the manufacturer's directions.

6. Knot the cords at both ends to prevent them from being pulled out. From one end, pull all the cords at once to gather the curtain panel to its determined finished width. Adjust the fullness evenly along the cords.

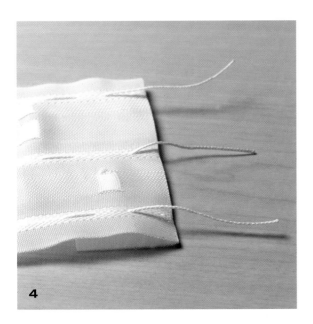

4

5

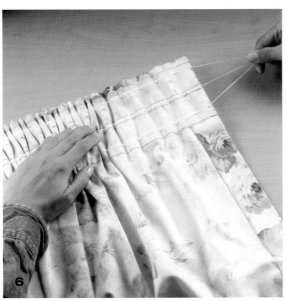

6

8

7. Knot the cords securely at the side. Wind the excess cord around a square of thin cardboard, and tuck it into the space between the tape and the curtain.

8. Hang the curtain using hooks through the woven-in loops on the tape. Or attach sew-on or clip-on rings, evenly spaced, along the upper edge.

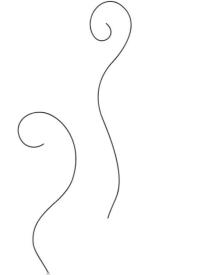

more ideas

ABOVE: Pencil pleat styling tape stitched along the sides of two queen-size sheets transforms them into a dramatic window treatment. The decorative top hems of the sheets become bold borders down the center of the window.

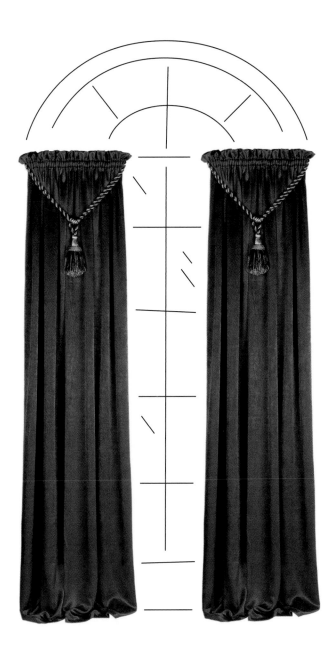

ABOVE: Shirring tape applied to the rod pocket of ready-made curtain panels gives them a more refined look. Elegant tasseled tiebacks draw eyes upward to get the full effect of a tall Palladian window.

RIGHT: Long floral tablecloths are transformed into bishop sleeve side panels simply by stitching smocking tape along one end. The panels are gathered up with Velcro ties, bloused out, and secured to cup hooks or tieback holders on the window frame.

shades

roman shade

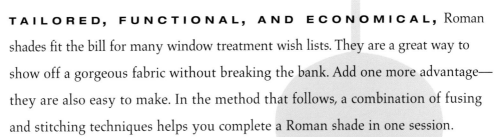

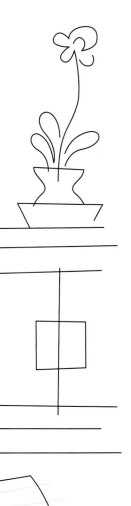

TAILORED, FUNCTIONAL, AND ECONOMICAL, Roman shades fit the bill for many window treatment wish lists. They are a great way to show off a gorgeous fabric without breaking the bank. Add one more advantage—they are also easy to make. In the method that follows, a combination of fusing and stitching techniques helps you complete a Roman shade in one session.

Cords strung through evenly spaced columns of small rings on the back of the shade allow it to be raised into soft folds. The number and placement of the ring columns determine the look of the shade as it is raised. The farther apart the rings are vertically, the deeper will be the folds. For lightweight shades up to 36" (91.5 cm) wide, columns of rings up the sides and in the middle are often all that is needed. For larger windows or heavy fabric, additional columns of rings will ensure smooth operation of the shade.

The keys to success when making Roman shades are to measure accurately and cut the fabric squarely. If you are making a shade for a bedroom, select tightly woven, mediumweight fabric and add a layer of light-blocking drapery lining to protect the shade from fading and to provide light control. For windows where there is less concern for privacy or light control, lightweight and semisheer fabrics can be used, but the rings and cords may show through.

If the window frame is deep enough to accommodate a 1 × 2 mounting board without compromising the functioning of the window itself, mount the shade inside the frame, with the front of the shade flush with the front of the frame. Otherwise, make the shade 2" (5 cm) wider than the window frame and mount the shade centered over the top of the window molding.

HOW TO MAKE A *roman shade*

MATERIALS

- Fabric

- Drapery lining, optional

- Paper-backed
  fusible adhesive,
  3/4" (2 cm) wide

- Thread

- Plastic rings

- Thin nylon cord

- 1 × 2 mounting board
  (page 132)

- Screw eyes

- Two 1" (2.5 cm) angle
  irons for outside mount

- Screws for mounting

- Flat metal weight bar,
  1/2" (1.3 cm) wide, or 1/4"
  (6 mm) wooden dowel,
  cut 1/2" (1.3 cm) shorter
  than finished shade width

- Awning cleat

- Staple gun and staples

- Drapery pull, optional

1. Measure (page 126) the window frame. Cut a 1 × 2 mounting board 2" (5 cm) longer than the outside measurement for an outside-mounted shade; cut the board 1/2" (1.3 cm) shorter than the measurement for an inside-mounted shade. Cover the mounting board (page 132); install the board (page 134) if it is an outside mount.

2. Determine the finished length of the shade. For an outside mount, measure from the top of the mounting board to the sill or 1/2" (1.3 cm) below the apron. For an inside mount, measure the inside frame to the sill. The finished width of the shade is equal to the board length plus 1/4" (6 mm). Add 7" (18 cm) to the finished length to determine the cut length of the fabric; add 2" (5 cm) to the finished width to determine the cut width. Cut the fabric, using a carpenter's square for accuracy. Cut lining, if desired, with the width equal to the finished width and the length equal to the finished length plus 3 1/2" (9 cm).

3. Press under 1" (2.5 cm) hems on the sides of the shade. Turn back the hems and fuse strips of 3/4" (2 cm) paper-backed fusible adhesive the length of each side, near the cut edge.

4. If lining the shade, place the lining over the shade, wrong sides together, with the lower edge of the lining 3 1/2" (9 cm) above the lower edge of the shade; tuck the lining under the side hems. Remove the protective paper backing from the fusible adhesive, and fuse the hems in place.

5. Press under 1/2" (1.3 cm) at the lower edge; then press under 3" (7.5 cm) to form the lower hem and weight bar pocket. Stitch in place.

6. On the shade back, draw a line across the top at the finished length. Cut off excess fabric 1 1/2" (3.8 cm) above the line, and finish the edges together with a zigzag or serged stitch.

7. Stitch rings to the back of the shade in an arrangement suitable for the shade weight and dimensions. Space columns evenly, with outer columns 3/4" (2 cm) from the outer edges. Space rows evenly 6" to 10" (15 to 25.5 cm) apart, from the top of the hem pocket to the top line. When raised, the shade will fall into folds half as deep as the space between rings. (Do not stitch rings along the top line.)

8. Insert the weight bar into the pocket; slipstitch or fuse the ends closed. Staple the shade to the mounting board, aligning the line on the shade to the top front edge of the board.

9. Insert screw eyes on the underside of the board, aligning them to the ring columns.

10. Cut a cord for each ring column 1½ times the shade length plus the distance from the column to the draw side. Tie cords to the bottom rings and string them up through the rings and screw eyes. Install the shade (page 134 and 135). With the shade lowered, knot cords together outside the last screw eye. Install an awning cleat on the frame or wall to hold the shade in place when raised.

RING ARRANGEMENT

↓ FINISHED LENGTH   ↕ 1½"

6" TO 10"

HEM

more ideas

RIGHT: Ready-made Roman shades are very plain, usually white or ivory in color. Scattered leaves were printed (page 104) onto this one to give it more character. This method of painting is very forgiving; the overlapping images and differences in intensity help create depth and interest.

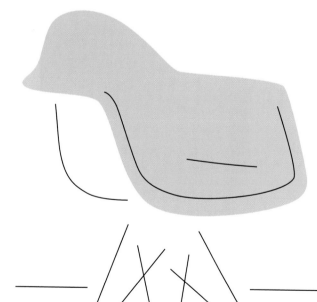

ABOVE: Create a cloud shade from a purchased rod-pocket curtain panel. Stitch rings in five evenly spaced columns to the back of the panel. Mount the panel on a curtain rod or tension rod, distributing the fullness evenly. Insert screw eyes directly into the inside top of the window frame. Cut a 1/4" (6 mm) wooden dowel weight bar the same width as the curtain rod, and insert small cup hooks into the ends. When stringing the shade, tie the two outer cords to the cup hooks and tie the three inner cords at even spaces along the bar.

roller shades

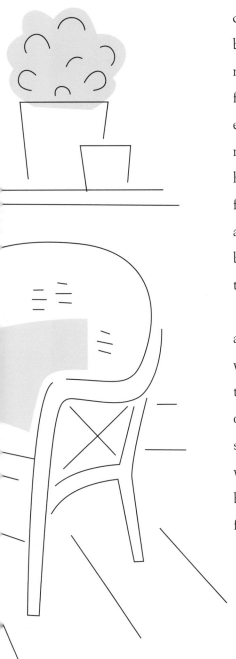

THIS NOSTALGIC HOME décor staple is making a comeback in many colorful ways. When fused to room-darkening backing, a roller shade provides optimum privacy and light control, making it an excellent choice for a bedroom or any window that faces the sun or a busy street. Designer details like a shaped bottom edge, decorator trim, or a clever handle make a big impact with minimal time and effort. Kits that include the roller, mounting hardware, and fusible backing help you make roller shades from the fabric of your choice without ever taking a stitch. Some kits include a pulley system for raising and lowering the shade; others operate by means of a spring inside the roller. The kit may also include a template for shaping the lower edge of the shade.

Ideally the shade should be mounted inside the window frame, as long as the frame is deep enough and the shade will not interfere with the operation of the window. Otherwise it can be mounted on the wall above and outside the frame. If the shade wraps off the back of the roller, it will hug the window more closely, cutting down on side light. The backing will be visible on the roller, so you will also want to plan a top treatment. For accuracy, the hardware should be mounted before you cut the shade to its final size. Be sure to allow for the diameter of the rolled shade when mounting the hardware.

HOW TO MAKE A *roller shade*

MATERIALS

- Roller shade kit that includes adjustable roller, mounting brackets, fusible backing, and hem slat

- Fabric

- Iron; large flat pressing surface

- Carpenter's square

- Fusible adhesive strip, if not included in shade kit

- Decorative trim

- Masking tape or vinyl tape

- Liquid fray preventer or fabric glue and small brush

1.   Install the mounting brackets and roller, and measure the roller to determine the finished width of the shade. Steam-press the fabric thoroughly to prevent shrinkage during fusing. Cut the fabric 2" (5 cm) wider and 14" (35.5 cm) longer than the desired finished size. Cut the backing 1" (2.5 cm) wider and 12" (30.5 cm) longer than the desired finished size.

2.   Press a crease across the fabric 6" (15 cm) from the lower edge, wrong sides together. Press the lower flap down again 1¹/₂" (3.8 cm) from the first crease, forming the hem stick pocket. Using a ³/₈" (1 cm) wide strip of fusible adhesive; fuse the upper edge of the pocket closed.

3.   Fuse the backing to the wrong side of the fabric, centering it on the width of the fabric. Use a press cloth and follow the manufacturer's directions.

4.   Mark the finished width on the shade backing. Square off the upper and lower edges, using a carpenter's square for accuracy. Draw a symmetrically shaped hem. Cut along the marked lines. Apply liquid fray preventer or diluted fabric glue along the cut edges, using a small paintbrush.

5.   Apply a decorative trim along the cut edge of the shaped hem, using fabric glue.

6.   Attach the shade to the roller, using masking tape or vinyl tape. In order for the shade to roll up properly, the upper edge must be square with the center of the roller. Attach the shade with the fabric facing up if you want the shade to roll off the front of the roller; attach it with the backing up if you want it to roll off the back of the roller.

7.   Trim the hem stick to fit the pocket; slide it into the pocket. Mount the roller shade on the brackets.

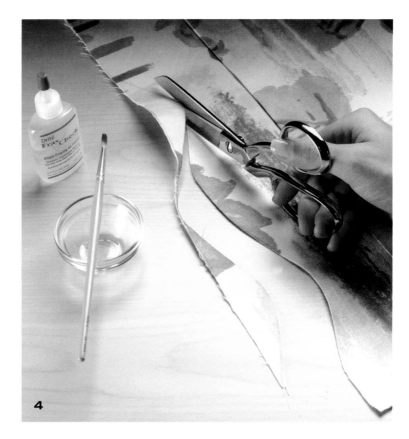

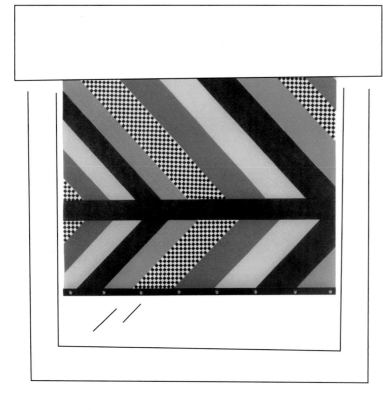

LEFT: A jazzy roller shade is made by fusing strips of tissue paper to the fusible backing. Instead of a hem pocket, the lower edge of the shade is sandwiched between two strips of $3/4$" (2 cm) pine screen molding, held together with small bolts and acorn caps (page 121).

BELOW: Oilcloth is simply cut to size and secured to the roller. A deep hem stick pocket is turned up at the lower edge and secured with grommets for a decorative peek-a-boo effect.

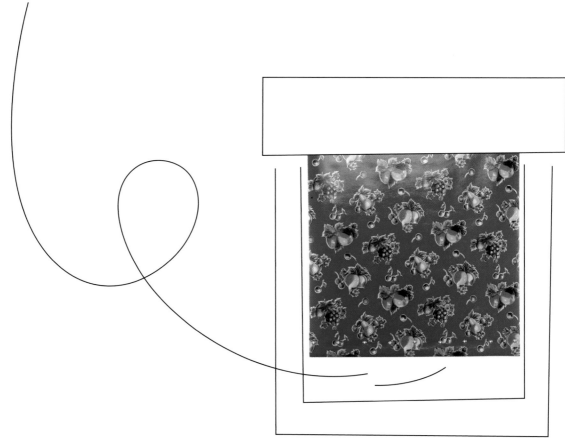

more ideas

ABOVE: An inexpensive purchased roller shade can be painted to fit the room décor, using opaque paint markers (page 108). Add a small painted knob, secured through the hem stick by means of a short hanger bolt.

RIGHT: Tabs and a painted wooden pole really spice up this roller shade. Follow the directions for making tabs on page 26, cutting the tab strips 3" × 4$^1/_2$" (7.5 × 11.5 cm). Turn 2" (5 cm) to the right side along the lower edge, and stitch $^3/_8$" (1 cm) from the fold, catching the tab ends and forming a facing. Press the facing to the back and fuse in place.

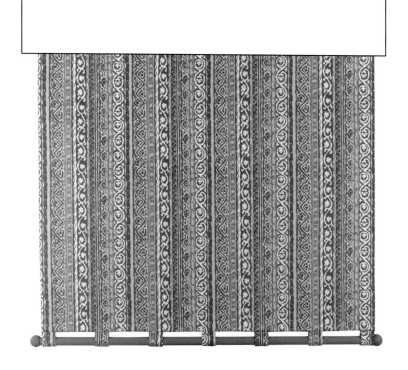

reverse roll-up shades

SHADES THAT ROLL up from the bottom have traditionally been raised by pulling cords that run through screw eyes and locking the cords around an awning cleat. This innovative version is raised and lowered by pulling or releasing two straps that are an integral part of the shade design.

With this method, two coordinating mediumweight fabrics are bonded together with paper-backed fusible web. One long strip of the fused fabrics flips over a mounting board at the top to form a self-valance and wraps around a wooden dowel at the bottom to form the roll. If the window receives strong light, avoid dark or bold colors that will fade noticeably. If show through is a concern, use a print fabric on the front and a solid fabric on the back to prevent shadowing of the fabric designs.

HOW TO MAKE A *reverse roll—up shade*

MATERIALS

- Two coordinating mediumweight fabrics

- Paper-backed fusible adhesive in a wide sheet

- Iron; large ironing surface

- Liquid fray preventer or fabric glue; small paintbrush

- Decorative trim

- Lightweight cotton strap, 1" (2.5 cm) wide; length equal to four times the shade length plus 12" (30.5 cm)

- Four 1" (2.5 cm) D-rings

- 1 × 4 mounting board

- Two angle irons; nuts and bolts for mounting board to the angle irons; screws for mounting the irons to the wall

- Awl

- Wooden dowel; 1/2" to 3/4" (1.3 to 2 cm) diameter

- Two round ball finials or drawer knobs

- Staple gun and staples

- Screws for mounting

1. Cut both fabrics and the fusible adhesive 1" (2.5 cm) wider than the desired finished size and 20" (51 cm) longer than the desired finished length. Fuse the adhesive to the wrong side of one of the fabrics; allow to cool. Remove the paper backing and fuse the second fabric to the first.

2. Mark the finished width on the shade. Square off the upper and lower edges, using a carpenter's square for accuracy. Draw a symmetrically shaped upper edge (this will become the bottom of the self-valance). Cut along the marked lines. Apply liquid fray preventer or diluted fabric glue along the cut edges, using a small paintbrush. Apply decorative trim to the valance edge, if desired.

3. Prepare the mounting board (page 132). Secure the angle irons to the back top of the board, using nuts and bolts. Mount the board; remove the board from the angle irons, leaving the irons on the wall.

4. Cut two straps about 4" (10 cm) longer than the valance; seal the ends with liquid fray preventer. Stitch two D-rings to one end of each strap. Staple the opposite strap ends in the desired positions to the top of the mounting board so they fall forward over the front.

5. Staple the shade over the top of the mounting board, allowing the desired length to hang forward for the valance. Pierce the fabric with an awl over the mounting holes.

6. Cut the remaining strap length in half; seal the ends. Staple one end of each strap to the top back of the mounting board, aligned to the front straps, so the long straps will fall behind the shade.

7. Cut the dowel to the shade width. Paint the dowel and knobs, if desired and allow to dry. Center the shade on the dowel, and staple in place, with the back side of the shade facing up. Roll the shade around the dowel until the shade is the desired finished length; staple again.

8. Mount the shade on the angle irons. Wrap the long straps under the dowel, up over the shade front, and through the D-rings. Pull on the straps to raise the shade.

1

4

7

more ideas

BELOW LEFT: This shade is made from a single layer of outdoor canvas fabric. The edges do not ravel when they are cut and the color is the same on front and back. The stenciled (page 102) valance for this shade was doubled back and stapled to the board so the right side would face out. The shade is secured in place with chain hooked to the center underside of the board. Vinyl-covered cup hooks, inserted into the dowel ends, hook into the chain links to keep the shade at the desired height.

BELOW RIGHT: A woven rag rug makes a colorful reverse roll-up shade. With the lower edge rolled tightly around the extra-long dowel, the lower fringes are pulled through to the rug back, using a crochet hook, and knotted to make a tight pocket. The shade is rolled to the desired height and held in place by resting the dowel ends on pegs, installed at the sides of the window frame.

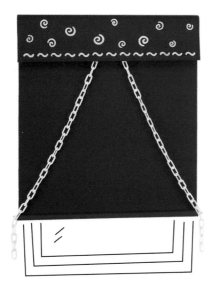

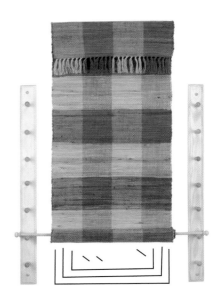

tent flap shade

FLAT, LINED PANELS attached to a mounting board open and close like a tent flap—thus the name. Variations in the way the shade is secured open offer several different looks. One panel can be drawn back from a corner or from partway up one side. Two slightly overlapping panels can be mounted side by side and drawn apart in the center. Separate panels made to fit individual frames in a bank of windows can be drawn open in symmetrical or asymmetrical patterns. The shade can be held open by slipping a buttonhole, grommet, or metal ring over a button, cup hook, or small wall hook.

The front and lining are both decorator fabrics because they are both visible when the shade is open. If the window receives strong light, avoid dark or bold colors for the lining because they may fade noticeably. If you decide to use two print fabrics, layer them and hold them up to the light to see if the design from the back fabric will shadow onto the front fabric. You may need to add plain drapery lining between the fabrics to prevent this.

HOW TO MAKE A *tent flap shade*

1. Cover and mount the mounting board (page 132). Measure from the top back of the mounting board to the the desired finished length; add 1/2" (1.3 cm) to determine the cut length of each piece. Measure the front and sides of the mounting board; add 1" (2.5 cm) to determine the cut width of each piece. Cut the pieces, including a piece of drapery lining, if interlining is necessary. Skip step 2, if interlining is not necessary.

2. Pin interlining to the wrong side of the shade front piece. Stitch together 3/8" (1 cm) from the outer edges. Repeat for any additional panels.

3. Pin the front and lining wrong sides together. Stitch together 1/2" (1.3 cm) from the edges along the sides and bottom, leaving the upper edge open for turning. Trim the seam allowances diagonally at the corners. Press the seam allowances open. Repeat for any additional panels.

4. Turn the panel(s) right side out. Press the outer edges. Zigzag or serge the upper edges together. Insert a buttonhole or grommet or hand-stitch a metal ring near a lower corner.

5. Center the shade on the mounting board, aligning the upper edge to the board back and wrapping the sides around the board ends. Staple the panel(s) to the mounting board, mitering out fullness at the corners.

6. Install hook(s) into the wall alongside the window frame at the desired height. Or sew a button to the side of the shade. Behind the button, attach a small piece of Velcro to secure it to the side of the window frame.

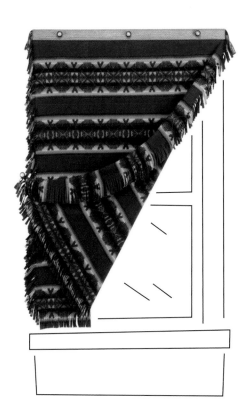

more ideas

ABOVE: Make a tent flap shade from a rectangle of polyester fleece. Fringe the edges for a rustic effect—cut edges on fleece do not ravel. Instead of conventional hardware, mount the shade using a quilt hanging rack. Install a drawer knob (page 120) alongside the window frame for tying the shade open.

RIGHT: Make the shade to fit the window dimensions. Install a grommet in each upper corner. Mount the shade to the window over small hooks installed in the upper corners of the window frame. Install a third hook partway up one side for pulling back the "tent flap."

top treatments

custom-fit swags

SWAGS THAT FRAME the window, dipping gracefully into single or multiple swoops and poufs, don't just happen by throwing a straight length of fabric over a rod or through some holders. Experienced decorators know how to manipulate the fabric to get the look they want, but it takes practice and patience. Some of the shaping can be done beforehand to make the styling process easier. With an understanding of some basic geometry and a clear idea of your intended design, you can accurately gauge the fabric length needed and be successful the first time you try.

To begin with, select a fabric that is soft, lightweight, and drapable. Neat narrow selvages can be used as the finished edges, eliminating the need for sewing or fusing lengthy side hems. The swag can be styled so the selvages never show. Then sketch your idea on paper so you will know how to measure the window. Using the method that follows, you can design swags with single or multiple swoops. Poufs or large, loose knots of fabric can be worked in at the upper corners or between swoops, and the sides can fall to the same or different lengths, hanging free, or breaking or puddling on the floor. If you can decide what you want, you can make it happen.

HOW TO MAKE A *custom swag with a single swoop*

MATERIALS

- String
- Tape measure
- Lightweight, drapable fabric, length determined in step 4
- Thread and sewing machine or fusible adhesive and iron
- Decorative pole and brackets or swag holders
- Velcro strap or twill tape for bundling fabric and securing to pole or holders
- Safety pins
- Double-sided carpet tape, for securing swag to pole

1. Mount a pole just above and even with the outer edges of the window frame. If using swag holders, position them at the upper frame corners. Drape a length of string over the pole or holders, following the desired line of the upper edge. (It may stretch straight across the top of the window or dip slightly). Continue the string to the desired finished lengths at the sides. This will be the finished length on the upper edge of the swag.

2. Drape a second string over the pole or holders, dipping to the lowest points desired for the centers of the swags and falling to the desired finished lengths at the sides. This will be the finished length of the lower edge of the swag. Mark both tapes where they meet on the pole or at the holders.

3. Measure and record the lengths of the strings for each section. Measurement A is from the long left point to the holder. Measurement B is from the long right point to the holder. Measurement C is the distance across the pole or between holders, and Measurement D is the length of the swoop between holders.

4. Cut the full width of the fabric with the length equal to Measurement A plus Measurement B plus Measurement D plus 2" (5 cm) for 1/2" (1.3 cm) double-fold bottom hems. For ends that puddle on the floor, add 15" (38 cm) for each puddle; for ends that just break at the floor, add 4" (10 cm) for each break.

5. Turn under and stitch or fuse 1/2" (1.3 cm) double-fold hems at the ends of the fabric length (page 141). For ends that puddle on the floor, the hem is not necessary.

6. Measure from the left end of the fabric a distance equal to Measurement A; mark both selvages with a small safety pin. Repeat on the right end, measuring a distance equal to Measurement B.

7. Subtract Measurement C from Measurement D; divide the result in half. Mark points on the upper edge of the center section this distance inward from the first marks. (The distance between points should equal Measurement C.) Draw light diagonal pencil or chalk lines from these points to the marks on the lower selvage.

8. Fanfold the swag along the marked lines, keeping the number and depth of folds consistent; secure with a Velcro strap or twill tape.

9. Hang the swag over the pole or holders; tie or pin to holders. Use carpet tape to secure the upper edge to the pole or window frame top as necessary for a straight upper edge. Style the folds in the swag and down the sides. For ends that puddle, bundle and tie the fabric end, flip it under, and arrange fabric around the bundle.

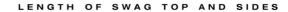

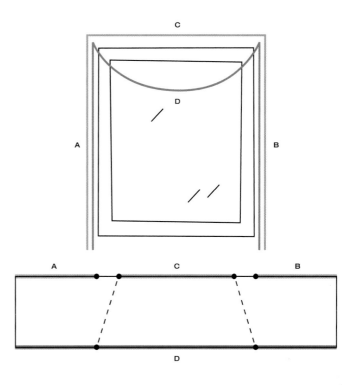

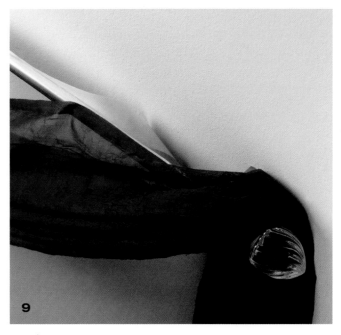

HOW TO MAKE A *swag with multiple swoops*

1. Mount the hardware and drape two strings. If the swoops are evenly spaced and of equal depth (opposite, top), record one measurement along the upper edge of the swoops and another measurement as the combined total of all the lower edges. Subtract the upper length from the lower length and divide the difference among the swoops; mark as shown in the diagram. If the swoops are spaced differently or are of different depths (opposite, bottom), take separate measurements for each swoop and mark as shown.

2. Mark the diagonal lines as in step 7, page 62. Fanfold and tie as in step 8. Hang and style the swag.

SWOOPS: EQUAL SPACE AND DEPTH

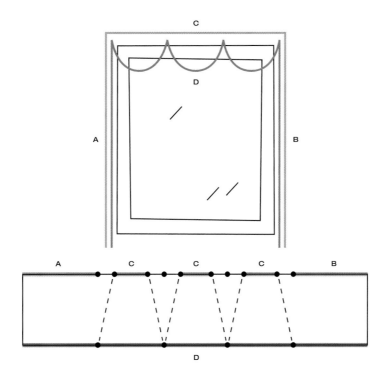

SWOOPS: DIFFERENT SPACE AND DEPTH

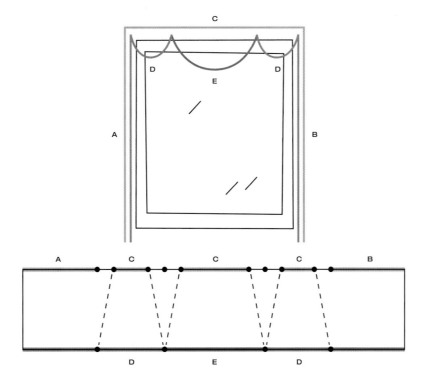

SWAG WITH CENTER POUF

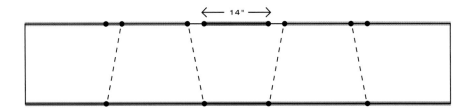

1. Mount the hardware and drape two strings as for single or multiple swoops. Allow 14" (35.5 cm) for each pouf when calculating the total length needed.

2. Determine the differences between upper and lower edges. Mark light pencil lines across the fabric to shape the swoops, leaving 14" (35.5 cm) spaces between lines if the swoops are to be divided by a pouf.

3. Fanfold along each marked line, keeping the number and depth of folds consistent; secure with Velcro straps or twill tape.

4. Tie adjacent bundles together to the same holder or at the same location on the rod, allowing the fabric between them to fall forward. Open the fabric to form a pouf, and style as desired.

HOW TO MAKE A *swag with a knot*

1. Follow steps 1 to 3, opposite, allowing 14" (35.5 cm) for each knot. Tie fabric between bundles into a large, loose knot over the rod or holder, pin adjacent bundles together inside the knot. If the treatment has multiple knots, begin in the center and work out toward each side.

more ideas

ABOVE: Hang a purchased swag over the front of a set of coordinating tab curtains. Begin by centering the swag through the two center tabs, and crossing the tails to opposite sides. Then run the swag tails through the outer tabs on both panels. To make styling easier, fanfold at the locations where the tails go through the tabs. Safety pin the upper edge of the swag to the tabs, and gently coax the lower edges of the swoops into position. Then safety pin the lower edges in place.

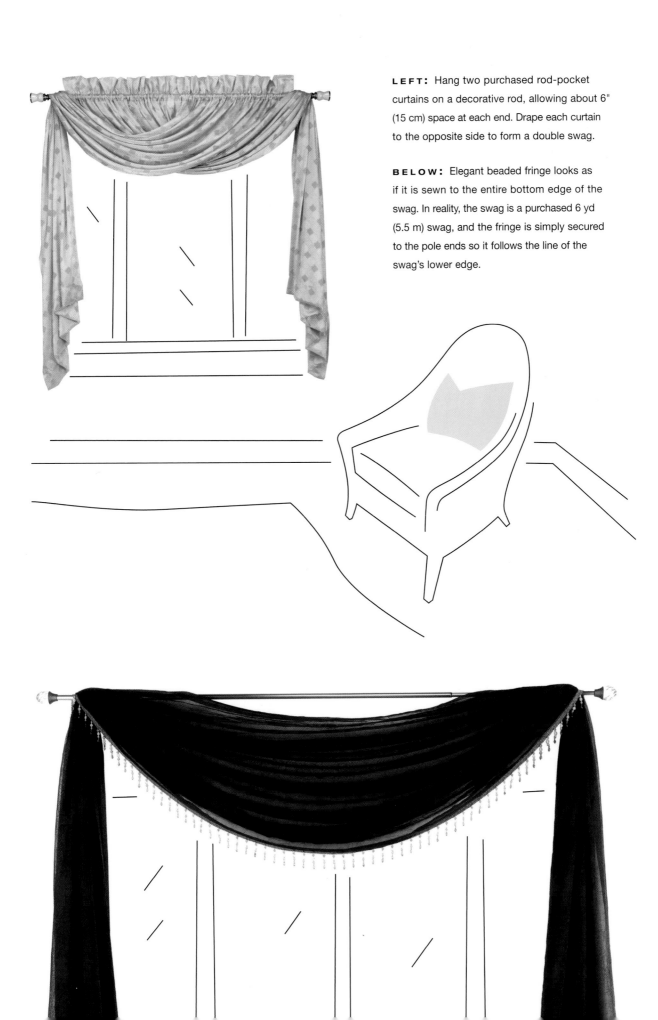

LEFT: Hang two purchased rod-pocket curtains on a decorative rod, allowing about 6" (15 cm) space at each end. Drape each curtain to the opposite side to form a double swag.

BELOW: Elegant beaded fringe looks as if it is sewn to the entire bottom edge of the swag. In reality, the swag is a purchased 6 yd (5.5 m) swag, and the fringe is simply secured to the pole ends so it follows the line of the swag's lower edge.

lined-to-the-edge panels

A VARIETY OF different looking treatments are created from the same simple technique of making a lined-to-the-edge rectangle of fabric. Differences in dimensions, how the panels are manipulated, and the methods of mounting them at the window are the factors that create a variety of distinctive styles.

Lined-to-the-edge panels are constructed from two coordinating decorator fabrics because both sides may be visible from the room. Often the treatment is wider than 54" (137 cm), the standard width of decorator fabric. If that is the case, select a fabric that can be railroaded—turned sideways with selvages running horizontally—to avoid unsightly vertical seams.

To determine the total length needed for the treatment shown, add twice the distance from the mounting board to the floor plus the mounting board width plus 20" (51 cm) to allow the ends to trail on the floor. Purchase half this amount of two fabrics; cut each in half lengthwise and stitch the pieces back together end to end in the center.

HOW TO MAKE A *lined-to-the-edge rectangle window treatment*

MATERIALS

- Two coordinating decorator fabrics; equal amounts of each, as determined in step 1.

- Thread

- Carpenter's square

- Paper-backed fusible adhesive, 3/8" (1 cm) wide

- Mounting board or decorative rod

1. Determine the necessary finished width and length of the flat panel as described in each caption. Add 1" (2.5 cm) to each dimension to determine the cut width and length. Railroad the pieces, if necessary. Cut identical pieces of both fabrics. If interlining is desired to prevent show through (page 55), cut it to the same size as the outer fabrics.

2. Pin the fabrics right sides together. If interlining is desired, place it over the pieces; pin around the outer edge. Stitch around the outer edge, using 1/2", seam allowances; leave a 10" (25.5 cm) opening for turning. Clip the outer corners diagonally.

3. Press the seam allowances open. Press back the seam allowances of the opening 1/2" (1.3 cm). Fuse a 10" (25.5 cm) strip of fusible adhesive over the seam allowance of the opening, following the manufacturer's directions.

4. Turn the rectangle right side out through the opening; press. Remove the protective paper backing from the fusible adhesive strip; fuse the opening closed.

5. Mount the rectangle to a fabric-covered board (page 132) or decorative rod over the window. For the treatment on page 70, secure the center to the mounting board with a fabric strap (page 26) and style the sides to drape dramatically.

2

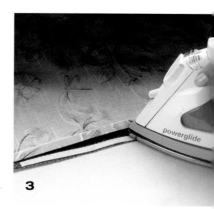

3

another idea

Narrow ribbon ties are simply run through king-size pillowcases and tied to crane rods in a little girl's bedroom. Pillow cases turned sideways are stapled to a mounting board and drawn up with ribbon in the center.

more ideas

OPPOSITE TOP: Mount a narrow decorative rod, $^1/2$" to $^3/4$" (1.3 to 2 cm) in diameter, over the window. Plan on a finished width equal to twice the length of the rod and a finished length of 15" to 18" (38 to 46 cm). Mark the upper edge at the ends and at intervals of approximately 16" (40.5 cm). Lay the rod over the upper edge of the valance. Pull the center mark over the rod, bunching the fabric together and pulling in about 4" (10 cm) on either side of the mark. Wrap and tie an 18" (46 cm) ribbon length around the fabric. Repeat at each mark.

OPPOSITE BOTTOM: A lined-to-the-edge table runner makes an instant top treatment. A rod is inserted through small slits cut in the lining.

LEFT: For a young boy's room, select two fabrics that have a "motorhead" theme. Make a lined rectangle 16" to 20" (40.5 to 51 cm) long and one-and-one-half times the window width wide. Fold down a 4" (10 cm) cuff along the upper edge and hang the topper from a narrow black rod using miniature clamps from the hardware store.

flip toppers

FLAT FABRIC PANELS that flip over decorative rods
are inexpensive and very easy to make, yet offer unlimited possibilities
for creative designs. As decorative accents over shades or blinds,
these toppers are simply lined-to-the-edge panels sewn from two
contrasting or coordinating fabrics. Cleverly used buttons and
buttonholes or grommets and ties secure the topper and add interesting
splashes of color. A layer of interlining is sandwiched between the
front and back fabrics to add body and support for the buttonholes.

Because you first create a paper pattern, you can design your
topper with straight, curved, or pointed lower edges. Sometimes a
printed fabric design will offer inspiration for the topper shape.
If your topper must be wider than the standard decorator fabric width,
look for fabric with a nondirectional print that can be railroaded
(page 71) to avoid unsightly vertical seams.

HOW TO MAKE A *flip topper*

1. Mount the rod just above and to the outside of the window frame. If there is an existing undertreatment, there should be ample clearance between it and the back of the rod. Measure from bracket to bracket to determine the pattern width. Hang a tape measure over the rod to determine the pattern length, as shown in the diagram.

PATTERN LENGTH

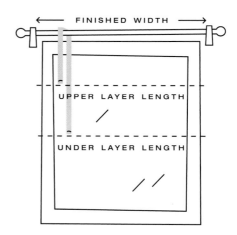

2. Cut a paper pattern; shape the lower edges as desired. Hang the pattern over the rod to check the fit and shape. Draw a line where the pattern crosses the rod. Measure the total pattern length and buy equal amounts of two fabrics and lining. Preshrink all three fabrics (page 136) if you intend to launder the topper.

3. Pin the pattern over one of the fabrics. The outer edge of the pattern is the stitching line for the topper. Mark the cutting line on the fabric 1/2" (1.3 cm) beyond the pattern edge. Cut out the fabric. Remove the pattern.

4. Place the other fabric face-up over the interlining. Pin the cut fabric face-down over both layers, aligning all grainlines. Cut the other layers, leaving the pins in the fabric.

5. Stitch around the outer edge, using 1/2" (1.3 cm) seam allowances; leave a 10" (25.5 cm) opening for turning. Clip the outer corners diagonally; clip up to, but not through, the stitching at inner corners and on curves.

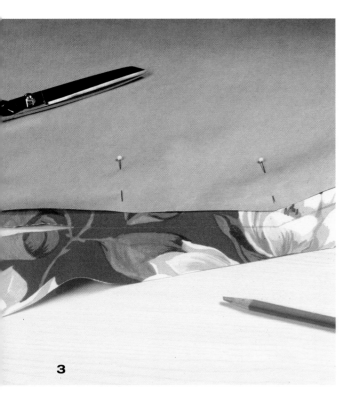

3

6

6. Press the seam allowances open. Press back the seam allowances of the opening 1/2" (1.3 cm). Fuse a 10" (25.5 cm) strip of fusible adhesive over the seam allowance of the opening, following the manufacturer's directions.

7. Turn the topper right side out through the opening; press. Remove the protective paper backing from the fusible adhesive strip; fuse the opening closed.

8. Fold the topper front down, using the line drawn on the pattern as a guide. Mark for the placement of buttonholes or grommets. Sew buttonholes and cut them open. Or insert grommets, following the manufacturer's directions.

9. Refold the topper. Mark the placement for buttons or ties on the lower layer. Sew on buttons or ties. Flip the topper over the rod and secure.

more ideas

RIGHT TOP: Soft pleats were folded in the bias direction on a square Hardanger embroidery tablecloth before flipping it over a rod. Carpet tape invisibly holds it in place.

RIGHT BOTTOM: A small sueded hide flipped over an iron rod is secured with leather lacing run through holes in metal conchos. Look for conchos in stores that carry other leather crafting supplies.

OPPOSITE TOP: A round tablecloth was flipped over a rod and tied up with ribbons for a feminine look.

OPPOSITE BOTTOM: Kitchen towels turned sideways are secured to a wood pole using carpet tape. The lower edges are pulled up in fan shapes and held in place with wired faux fruit clusters.

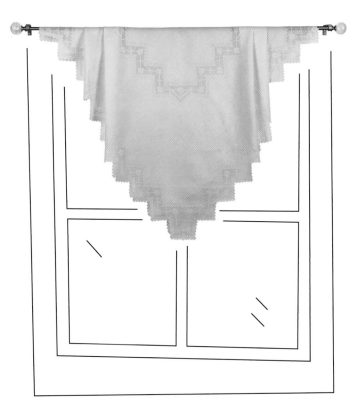

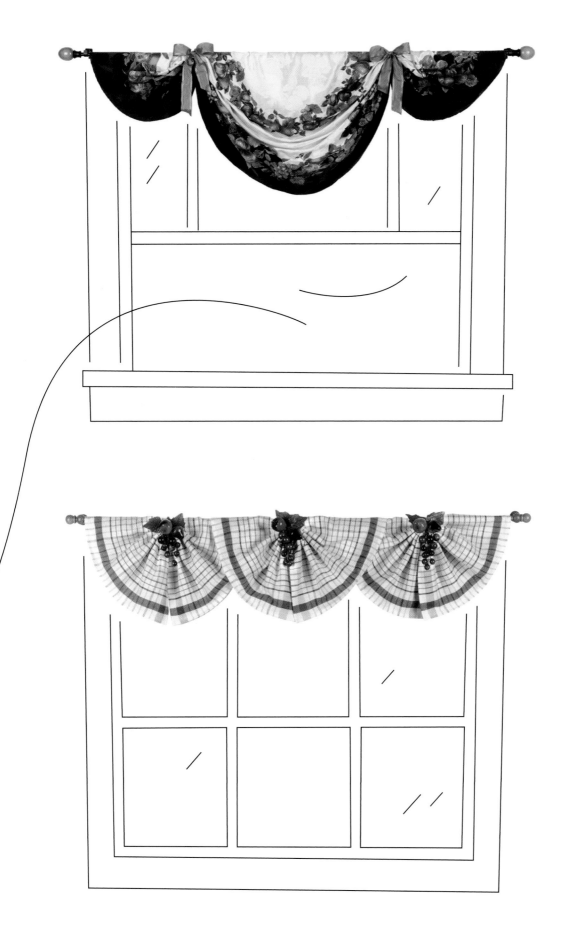

triangle swags

SLEEK CONTEMPORARY STYLING
doesn't get much easier than this. A square of decorator
fabric is folded in half diagonally and stitched to make a
self-lined triangle. The points are pulled through small
metal rings and secured to hooks on the window frame,
allowing the bias grain to fall in soft, deep folds. As an
optional accent, you can dangle crystals, beads, feathers, or
tassels from the center point of the triangle swag.

The original size of the fabric square determines
the finished size of the triangle. The size and appearance of
the swag is also altered by the amount of fabric that is
pulled through the rings at the sides and by the distance
between hooks. For instance, a swag made from a 45"
(114 cm) square can be made to fit a window width of
36" to 45" (91.5 to 114 cm) simply by pulling more or
less fabric through the rings. Several small swags can be
overlapped to make a continuous valance for a wide
window, with overlapping points sharing the same rings.
To determine the spacing, size, and number of swags
that are right for your window, experiment with
triangles cut from old sheets or inexpensive fabric.

HOW TO MAKE A *triangle swag*

MATERIALS

- Decorator fabric

- Test fabric, such as muslin

- Carpenter's square

- Paper-backed fusible adhesive, 3/8" (1 cm) wide

- Metal rings, 1" (2.5 cm) diameter

- Thread

- Cup hooks

- Embellishments for swag points as desired

1. Cut a square of decorator fabric, using a carpenter's square to ensure right angles and equal sides. Fold the square in half diagonally, right sides together. Stitch 1/2" (1.3 cm) from the cut edges, leaving a 6" (15 cm) opening for turning.

2. Taper the seam allowances at the points; clip diagonally across the square corner. Press the seam allowances open. Press back the seam allowances of the opening 1/2" (1.3 cm). Fuse a 6" (15 cm) strip of fusible adhesive over the seam allowance of the opening, following the manufacturer's directions.

3. Turn the swag right side out through the opening; press the seamed edges. Do not press the bias fold. Remove the protective paper backing from the fusible ahesive strip; fuse the opening closed. Secure an embellishment to the center point, if desired.

4. Attach cup hooks to the upper corners of the window frame. Insert the swag points the desired distance through metal rings; hand-tack in place. Hang the rings on the hooks.

2

4

more ideas

LEFT: Over inside-mounted miniblinds or pleated shades, you can make the top treatment even easier. Fold a large square fashion scarf or small square tablecloth in half diagonally and tie the ends to coat hooks mounted outside the upper corners of the window frame.

BELOW: Dinner napkins are used to create a short but colorful valance in a breakfast nook. Ends are run through napkin rings that hang from the pole.

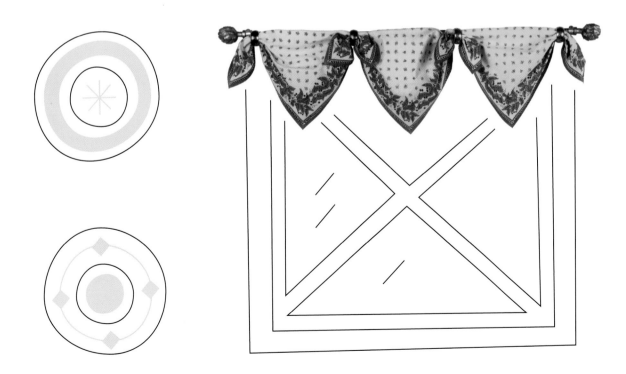

bias ruffle valance

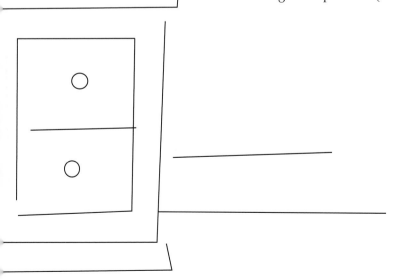

A BIAS RUFFLE is cut from a "donut" of fabric. The inner cut edge, with a shorter circumference, becomes the upper edge of the valance. The lower edge, with its much longer circumference, falls into soft ripples. This is a no-sew project; all the cut edges are either hemmed or covered with decorator trim, using fusible adhesive. The valance is attached to a decorative rod with clip-on rings.

One-and-one-half yards (1.4 m) of fabric 54" (137 cm) wide will yield a bias ruffle valance 12" to 15" (30.5 to 38 cm) long and up to 75" (190.5 cm) wide.

HOW TO MAKE A *bias ruffle valance*

MATERIALS

- 1¹/₂ yd (1.4 m) fabric, 54" (137 cm) wide

- Paper-backed fusible adhesive, ⁵/₈" (1.5 cm) wide

- Iron

- Decorator fringe; measure lower edge of valance to determine length needed

- Decorative rod and clip-on rings

1. Fold the fabric in half lengthwise and again crosswise; place on a flat surface. Using a string-and-pencil compass, secure the stationary end to the corner folds and mark an arc as close as possible to the selvages and cut ends. Then mark another arc a distance from the first one equal to the desired finished length of the valance plus 1" (2.5 cm). Cut on both lines through all the layers. Before unfolding the ring of fabric, cut one of the folds open.

2. Mount the rod. Determine how much of the bias ruffle you will need by clipping it to the rod. Allow slight fullness so the valance can form a soft ruffle. Cut off the excess. Turn under and fuse narrow single-fold hems in the cut ends of the ruffle.

3. Fuse a strip of paper-backed fusible adhesive to the right side of the ruffle, along the lower edge. Remove the paper backing, and fuse the heading of the decorator fringe over the adhesive.

4. Fuse a strip of paper-backed fusible adhesive to the wrong side of the ruffle, along the upper cut edge. Peel away the paper backing. Make small clips into the fabric every 1" (2.5 cm), about two-thirds into the fusible adhesive. Turn the edge under along the inner edge of the fusible adhesive and fuse in place, allowing the cut edge to spread along the clips.

5. Hang the valance from clip-on rings, spacing the rings about 8" (20.5 cm) apart.

CUTTING GUIDE

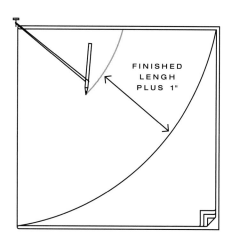

FINISHED LENGH PLUS 1"

another idea

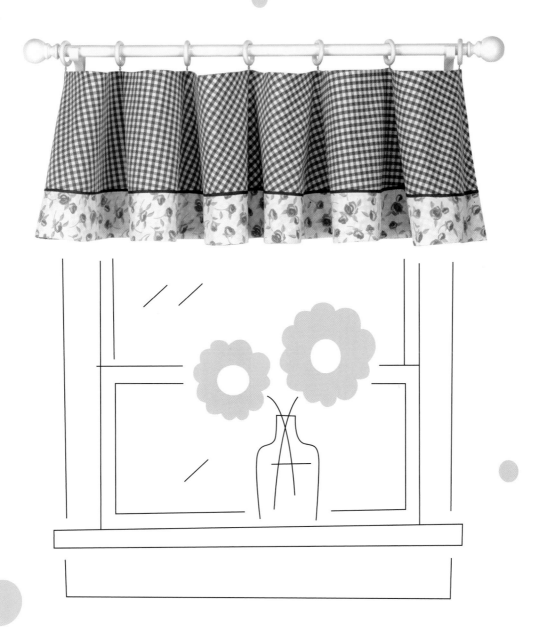

A ready-made round tablecloth becomes a bias ruffle valance, using only a scissors and fusible adhesive. The lower edge already has a neat hem; this one even has an applied border. A round tablecloth with a 70" to 72" (178 to 183 cm) diameter will produce a valance 12" to 15" (30.5 to 38 cm) long and up to 120" (305 cm) wide; enough for two average windows in the same room.

swag 'n' tails from lace tablecloth

FINISHED CURVED EDGES and a uniquely patterned lace design give this rod-pocket swag 'n' tails the look of an expensive, custom-made treatment. In reality, it began as a relatively inexpensive lace tablecloth. Because the outer edges are already shaped and finished, the only sewing required is stitching the rod pocket and the side hems.

The chart on page 93 lists some common oval tablecloth sizes and the window widths they will cover. The tails will be a few inches (centimeters) less than half the tablecloth length, after stitching the rod pocket. The swag length at the center will be few inches (centimeters) less than half the tablecloth width. If desired, the swag can be cut shorter, but it will also become slightly narrower.

HOW TO MAKE A *lace swag 'n' tails*

MATERIALS

- Oval lace tablecloth

- Curtain rod

- Steel tape measure; carpenter's square

- Thread

1. Cut the tablecloth in half lengthwise. Set aside one half for the swag panel. Cut the remaining piece in half crosswise for the two tails.

2. Press and stitch 1" (2.5 cm) double-fold hems (page 141) in the long cut edges of the tails.

3. Press under 1/2" (1.3 cm) on the upper edge of each tail panel. Then turn under the desired rod-pocket depth (page 18). Pin out excess fullness into small tucks as necessary. Stitch the rod pocket.

4. Repeat step 3 for the swag panel. Insert the curtain rod or pole through the rod pockets; mount the rod. Distribute the fullness evenly.

TABLECLOTH CUTTING GUIDE

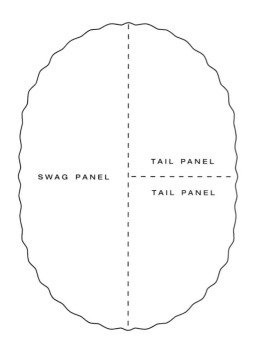

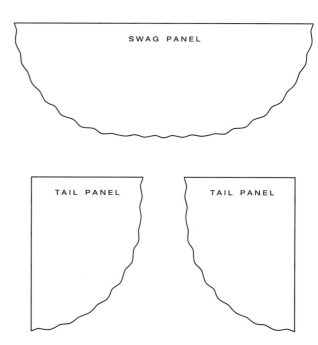

TABLECLOTH SIZE	WINDOW WIDTH
52" × 70" (132 × 178 cm)	45" to 68" (114 to 173 cm)
60" × 84" (152 × 213 cm)	56" to 80" (142 to 203 cm)
60" × 92" (152 × 234 cm)	59" to 85" (150 to 216 cm)
60" × 104" (152 × 264 cm)	64" to 91" (163 to 231 cm)
60" × 120" (152 × 305 cm)	75" to 104" (190 to 264 cm)

3

an idea

A banded rectangular tablecloth was cut up and turned into valance and side panels. Rather than sewing rod pockets at the top, the pieces were attached to pinch-pleat styling tapes (page 32).

board–mounted valances

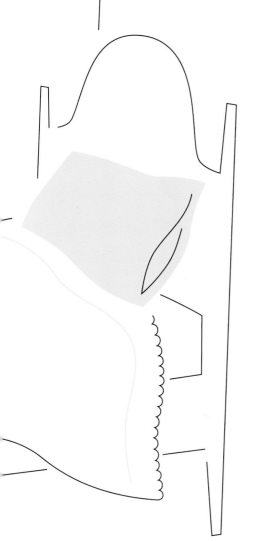

WITH A LITTLE imagination and inspiration, all sorts of common household materials, purchased linens, or art materials can be manipulated and secured to a mounting board to create an interesting top treatment. None of the ideas on the next four pages requires a sewing machine. If you can glue, you can do! Here eyelet valance fabric, available at most fabric stores, is simply glued to a mounting board and given a cheerful crown of daisies.

Nominal pine lumber works just fine for any of these ideas. In most cases, the wood will never show, so you don't even have to cover it with fabric (page 133) or paint it. Choose 1 × 4 pine if the treatment will be used alone or over an inside-mounted undertreatment. Use 1 × 6 pine to allow enough clearance if used over the top of an outside-mounted undertreatment. Before decorating the board, mount it to the wall, using simple angle irons; select a size with sides that are at least half the board width. Remove the board, leaving the angle irons on the wall. Later, it will be much easier to remount the treatment. See page 134 for more information about mounting boards.

HOW TO MAKE A *board-mounted valance*

MATERIALS

- Mounting board cut 2" (5 cm) longer than window frame or undertreatment width

- Angle irons and screws

- Eyelet valance fabric, 1½ to 2 times the board length plus twice the width

- Paper-backed fusible adhesive, 5/8" (1.5 cm) wide

- Iron

- Hot glue gun

- Staple gun

- Daisy garland

1. Fuse narrow single-fold hems in the short cut ends of the eyelet. Fuse a strip of the adhesive to the underside of the upper cut edge; remove the paper backing. Fold under the edge 4" (10 cm) and fuse in place; do not press the fold.

2. Divide the board edge, including ends, into eight even spaces; mark. Repeat for the valance, marking on the back side along the fused edge.

3. Apply hot glue along the board edge between the first two marks. Secure the valance to the board with the heading extending 4" (10 cm) above the board; gather the valance to fit the space. Repeat for each succeeding space.

4. Separate the layers of the heading to puff it out.

5. Secure the daisy garland to the board front over the gathers, using a staple gun.

6. Mount the valance on the angle irons.

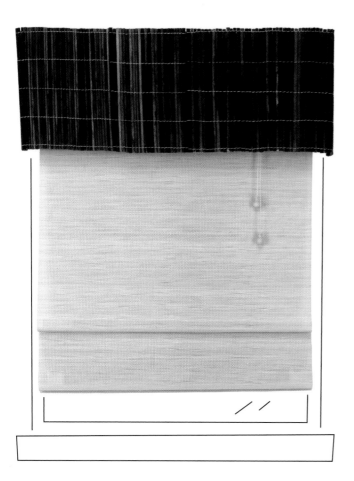

more ideas

TOP: Bamboo placemats are glued to the front and sides of a mounting board, using hot glue intended for wood. This is easier if you place the placemats on a flat surface, keeping them aligned along a straightedge. Then apply glue to the board and place it over the placemats just below one edge.

BOTTOM: Corrugated cardboard, secured to the board front with upholstery nailheads, takes on a soft, seasonal look with a garland of fall leaves.

5

more ideas

OPPOSITE: Dinner napkins, cut in half diagonally, are arranged in an overlapping pattern and stapled to the top of the mounting board.

RIGHT: Craft foam die-cut shapes are glued to larger sheets of foam secured to a mounting board to make a playful, inexpensive, kid's room accent.

BELOW LEFT: Fabric placemats in two colors are overlapped along the front and sides of a mounting board. Corners of the front layer are folded back with dots of hot glue to reveal the contrasting color underneath. Even the buttons are hot-glued on!

BELOW RIGHT: Colorful, kitchen towels with bold borders are cut to length, pleated along the stripes, and stapled to a mounting board. Staples are hidden under the knife pleats.

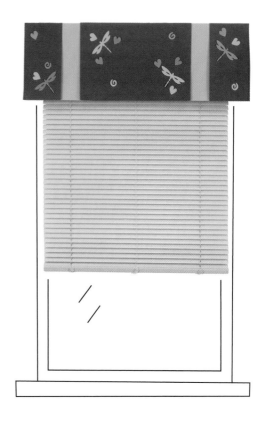

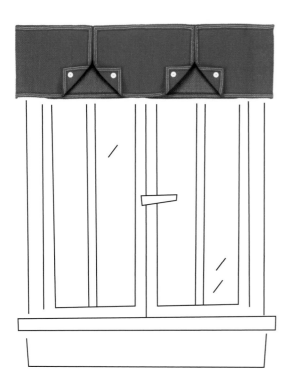

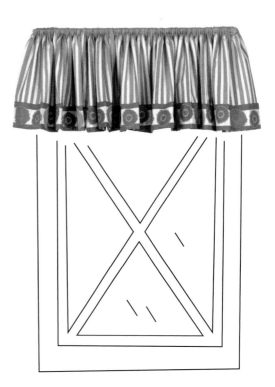

designer touches

stenciling

STENCILED DESIGNS GIVE plain, single-color fabrics or ready-made window treatments a custom look for your home. Craft stores and fabric stores carry a wide range of precut stencils. Some are a single plate for designs that are to be stenciled in one color. Others have more than one plate, numbered in sequence, to create multicolored images. For stenciling fabric, avoid stencils with minute details that will be distorted or lost by the fabric grain.

The clearest stenciled images are achieved on natural-fiber fabrics, such as cotton or linen, using opaque fabric paints. Acrylic craft paints can also be used; simply add fabric medium to the paints to ensure that the finished designs will last through laundering. Foam applicators or makeup sponges are useful for applying the paint over stencils that have relatively small design areas. Sponge rollers make quick work of covering large, open areas. If a dappled or shaded effect is desired, the paint can be applied with a damp sea sponge or cellulose sponge.

Reverse roll-up
shade (page 53).

HOW TO STENCIL ON A *window treatment*

MATERIALS

- Stencil

- Paint applicator as described opposite

- Opaque fabric paint or acrylic paint and fabric medium in desired colors

- Plastic drop cloth

- Masking tape

- Repositionable spray adhesive

- Iron; press cloth

1. Launder the fabric before making the window treatment, or launder ready-made treatments to remove any sizing from the fabric. Do not use fabric softener. Cover the work surface with a plastic drop cloth. Mark the desired locations for the stenciled images, using small pieces of masking tape. Stretch the finished window treatment taut, right side up, over the drop cloth. Clamp or tape the fabric in place.

2. Apply repositionable stencil adhesive to the back of the stencil, following the manufacturer's directions. Place the stencil on the fabric at the first mark. Press around the openings with your fingers. Mask off any openings that are not to be colored with the first paint color, using masking tape.

3. Pour a small amount of paint onto a paper plate; mix in fabric medium, if necessary, following the manufacturer's directions.

4. Dip the applicator into the paint; blot off the excess paint. Hold the applicator perpendicular to the fabric, and apply the paint using an up-and-down pouncing motion.

5. Lift the stencil and reposition it at the next mark. Apply all the stencils of the same color before switching to another stencil or masking off a different area.

6. For multi-plate stencils, allow the first color to dry before covering with the second stencil plate. Align the registration marks on the second plate to the painted sections. Stencil the second color. Repeat for any additional plates.

7. Allow the images to dry 24 hours. Heat-set the designs, using a dry iron and a pressing cloth.

nature printing

FRESH LEAVES ARE the perfect tools for creating leaf images on fabric. Select flat leaves that have interesting vein patterns. Experiment with the printing process on paper before applying the images to fabric to determine which leaves provide the desired results. Usually, printing with the back side of the leaf provides more detail in the print.

Use opaque or translucent fabric paints or acrylic craft paints mixed with fabric medium. Opaque paints give the most solid-looking, true-color image; translucent paints appear more sheer, and their colors are altered by the color of the fabric. The process is more durable on natural-fiber fabrics, such as cotton or linen, but will also work well on blends or synthetics if they will not be laundered.

Roman shade
(page 42).

HOW TO *nature print on fabric*

MATERIALS

- Plastic drop cloth

- Masking tape or clamps

- Fresh leaves

- Fabric paints or acrylic craft paints and fabric medium

- Wax paper

- Foam applicator

- Rubber brayer

1. Launder the fabric before making the window treatment, or launder ready-made treatments to remove any sizing from the fabric. Do not use fabric softener. Cover the work surface with a plastic drop cloth. Mark the desired locations for the printed images, using small pieces of masking tape. Stretch the finished window treatment taut, right side up, over the drop cloth. Clamp or tape the fabric in place.

2. Press the leaves flat by placing them between the pages of a large book for about an hour. Apply a thin layer of paint to the back side of a leaf, using a foam applicator.

3. Position the leaf, paint side down, over the fabric at the first mark; cover with a sheet of wax paper. Roll the brayer over the leaf to make the imprint. Carefully remove the wax paper and leaf. Repeat for each image.

4. Allow the prints to dry 24 hours. Heat-set the designs, using a hair dryer set on high or a dry iron and a pressing cloth.

stamping

LARGE FOAM RUBBER stamps are ideal for stamping images on fabric. Designs for kids' rooms can be found in crafts stores; more sophisticated designs are found with other wall décor items. You can also create your own stamps easily by cutting shapes from neoprene insulation strips or a rubber computer mouse pad and adhering them to an empty CD case.

As with other painting techniques, fabric paints or acrylic craft paints mixed with fabric medium work well for stamping. When stamping on colored fabric, best results are achieved with opaque paints; translucent paint colors are altered by the fabric color. The weave structure of the fabric plays a large part in the clarity of the design. Obviously, the clearest results are obtained on tightly woven fabric with fine yarns. The looser the weave and the larger the yarns, the more distorted the stamped image will be.

Tent flap shade
(page 57).

HOW TO *stamp on fabric*

MATERIALS

- Plastic drop cloth

- Masking tape or clamps

- Foam rubber stamp

- Fabric paints or acrylic craft paints and fabric medium

- Foam applicators

- Large, flat artist's eraser or printing block, available at art supply stores, and wipe-out tool for negative design stamping

1. Launder the fabric before making the window treatment, or launder ready-made treatments, if possible, to remove any sizing from the fabric. Do not use fabric softener. Cover the work surface with a plastic drop cloth. Stretch the finished window treatment taut, right side up, over the drop cloth. Clamp or tape the fabric in place.

2. Apply paint directly onto the stamp, using a foam applicator. For multicolored stamped designs, use small applicators and apply different colors to different areas of the stamp.

3. Press the stamp onto the fabric; lift the stamp straight up from the fabric. Repeat immediately once or twice in an area near the first image to create designs with varying intensities, depth, and shading. Or reapply paint before stamping again to create images with the same intensity.

negative design stamp

Brush paint onto the surface of an artist's eraser or printing block. Remove paint to create a negative design, using a wipe-out tool or pencil eraser. Stamp the design, following step 3 above.

Roller shade (page 49).

paint markers

OPAQUE PAINT MARKERS make quick, accurate work of painting multicolored designs on a variety of surfaces, including fabric, vinyl, paper, and wood. They are available in a nice assortment of brilliant colors in fine and medium points. When dry, the paints are permanent, lightfast, and waterproof. There are also paint markers designed specifically for working on fabric.

Mistakes are, unfortunately, permanent. The paints dry quickly to the touch and are not water soluble. Practice the painting technique on paper to become comfortable with the firmness of pressure needed and the amount of paint that flows from the marker tip. Shake the markers thoroughly before removing the caps, and replace the caps to shake the markers frequently during use.

HOW TO PAINT A DESIGN ON A *vinyl roller shade*

MATERIALS

- Vinyl roller shade

- Masking tape

- Smudgeproof transfer paper, ballpoint pen (optional)

- Design, enlarged to fit the desired space

- Opaque paint markers in desired colors

- Paper towels

1. Enlarge your chosen design to fit the shade. If you can see the design through the shade, tape the design to a flat work surface, and roll out the shade over the design. Otherwise transfer the design to the shade front, using smudgeproof transfer paper. Secure the shade edges to the surface, using masking tape.

2. Read and follow the paint marker manufacturer's directions. Keep paper towels handy for removing excess paint from the

marker points. Paint the design, beginning in the area farthest from you and working toward yourself to avoid smudging the paint.

3. Allow the paint to dry for at least 24 hours before rolling the shade—longer if working in humid conditions.

more painting ideas

Give plain-colored fabric or purchased window treatments visual texture by applying fabric paint with a texturizing paint roller, available in the paint department of home improvement centers. Texturize the entire fabric surface or apply the paint in stripes.

banding

BANDS OF FABRIC or ribbons applied to a window treatment accent the lines, define the shape, and create interesting perceptions. Colors used elsewhere in the room seem more apparent when they are repeated by banding on the window treatment. Vertical bands visually heighten the window, seemingly raising the ceiling and perhaps creating an aura of grandeur. Horizontal bands, on the other hand, widen the perceived window shape and draw the eye around the room. They may help to make a large room feel cozier.

While sewing is certainly an option, it can be time-consuming and could also create little annoyances like puckers and unsightly stitching lines. Fusible adhesives require only that you spend a little quality time with your iron. Paper-backed fusible adhesive, such as HeatnBond by Therm O Web, Inc. creates a very durable bond and a nice neat appearance. The strips are available in 10 yd (9.15 m) packages in widths of 3/8", 5/8", and 7/8" (1, 1.5, and 2.2 cm). Select a width equal to or slightly narrower than the ribbon width for banding with ribbons up to 1" (2.5 cm) wide or use the 3/8" (1 cm) width for wider ribbons and fabric bands.

Flat-panel
curtain (page 15).

HOW TO APPLY *fabric bands*

MATERIALS

- Fabric, ribbon, or flat decorative trim for banding
- Paper-backed fusible adhesive
- Iron

1. Mark light placement lines on the window treatment, using pencil. Determine the banding length and width desired. Cut fabric strips about 2" (5 cm) longer and 3/4" (2 cm) wider than the desired finished size. For best results, cut strips on the lengthwise grain of the fabric. Piece them together as necessary, either by stitching or fusing.

2. Adjust the iron temperature to the silk setting, without steam. Working from the roll, align 3/8" (1 cm) paper-backed adhesive on the right side of the banding to one outer edge. Slide the iron along the strip at a steady pace; the iron needs only to be in contact with the adhesive for about two seconds to create a temporary bond. Repeat on the opposite side. Then fuse a strip of adhesive to one end.

3. Press under along the inner edge of the adhesive strips, first on the long sides and then on the end. Allow to cool; remove the paper backing from the strips.

4. Align the banding to the placement lines. Beginning at the folded end, slide the iron along the band at a steady pace, keeping the iron in contact with each section for about six seconds.

mitered corner

Stop fusing as you approach the corner. Fold and finger-press the mitered corner; pin along the diagonal fold. On the underside, trim away the folded-out band to within 1/2" (1.3 cm) of the diagonal. Reposition the banding, remove the pins, and fuse in place. Slip a piece of adhesive under the diagonal fold and fuse in place.

HOW TO APPLY *ribbon or flat trim banding*

1. Mark light placement lines on the window treatment, using pencil. Determine the ribbon length needed, and cut the ribbon about 2" (5 cm) longer. Press under 1/2" (1.3 cm) at one end.

2. Adjust the iron temperature to the silk setting, without steam. Working from the roll, center the paper-backed fusible adhesive strip on the back side of the ribbon, aligning the strip end to the fold. Fuse in place to the end of the ribbon. For wide ribbon, apply a narrow strip of the adhesive to each outer edge. Allow the adhesive to cool.

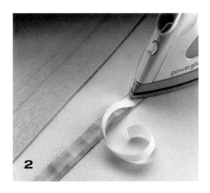

3. Peel off the paper backing. Align the ribbon, adhesive side down, to the marked lines. Beginning at the folded end, slide the iron along the ribbon at a steady pace, keeping the iron in contact with each ribbon section for about six seconds.

4. Stop fusing as you approach the end. Trim the ribbon 1/2" (1.3 cm) longer than the desired stopping point. Turn under the ribbon end and finish fusing. Fuse a 1/2" (1.3 cm) piece of adhesive to the underside of the ribbon end, and fuse in place.

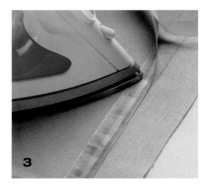

mitered corner

Stop fusing as you approach the corner. Fold and finger-press the mitered corner. Fuse in place. Continue. For wide ribbons, you may want to slip a short piece of adhesive under the diagonal fold and fuse in place.

Tab curtain
(page 28).

fused appliqués

FOR A QUICK and easy way to customize a plain curtain, shade, or top treatment, consider fused appliqués. Look for design ideas amid the countless paper die-cuts at the craft store, copyright-free design books, or even on the Internet, using the keyword: clipart.

For best results, arrange a row of appliqués above the lower hem of a curtain where they will not be distorted or lost in gathers. Or use appliqués on tent-flap shades, flip toppers, or lined-to-the-edge rectangles. Select fabric for the appliqués that coordinates well with the window treatment but creates enough of a contrast to be noticeable.

HOW TO APPLY fused appliqués

MATERIALS

- Paper-backed fusible adhesive in a sheet
- Lightweight to mediumweight fabric for appliqués
- Iron; press cloth

1. Trace the desired shapes onto the paper side of the fusible adhesive; for asymmetrical designs, trace the mirror image. Apply the fusible adhesive to the wrong side of the appliqué fabric, following the manufacturer's directions.

2. Cut out the designs. Remove the paper backing.

3. Arrange the appliqués on the completed window treatment. Fuse in place.

lining a treatment

ADDING LINING TO a window treatment adds to the expense and could tack on at least an extra hour of your time. But, you may find it's worth the effort. Besides giving the treatment extra body, lining also protects the fabric from sun fading, supports the side hems and headings of grommeted or rod-pocket curtains, and gives a uniform white or ivory appearance to the windows from the outside. Lining also reduces the outside light filtration through curtains or valances, reducing the visibility of seams and hems.

Select drapery lining fabric in the same width as the decorator fabric for the project, so that any seams will fall in the same location and the finished panels will be the same width. With these few additional steps, you can add lining to any of the flat-panel curtains, (page 10), relaxed or classic rod-pocket curtains (pages 16 to 23), tab curtains (page 24) or curtains made with self-styling tapes (page 30).

Flat-panel
curtain (page 10).

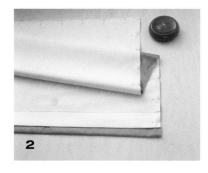

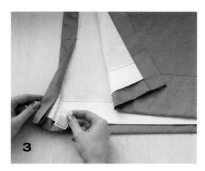

HOW TO LINE A *curtain*

1. Cut the lining fabric pieces 5" (12.5 cm) shorter than the curtain fabric pieces. Prepare the curtain up to the completion of the bottom hem. Follow the same steps for the lining, making a 2" (5 cm) double-fold bottom hem (page 141).

2. Pin the outer panel and the lining panel wrong sides together, matching the sides and upper edge. If one panel is wider than the other, trim off the excess fabric. At the bottom hems, the lining will be 1" (2.5 cm) shorter than the curtain.

3. Complete the curtain, handling both layers together as one fabric. Stitch through all the layers, catching the lining in the side hems and the stitching lines at the curtain top. Encase a drapery weight in the space between the layers of the lower hem before finishing the sides hems.

building body

To give silky, lustrous curtains an opulent look, decorators interline them with a thick, padding fabric that is usually not available at your local fabric store. The interlining and lining fabrics are stitched into the curtain panel, which requires careful measuring and some tedious sewing. However, you can create this appearance for stationary, flat-panel curtains with a free-hanging curtain liner made from a common flannel sheet. Purchase a white or off-white flat flannel sheet in a size closest to the finished size of the curtain panel, and rehem the sheet to match the size of the curtain. Then hang the sheet and curtain together as one from clip-on hooks.

decorator trims

THERE'S NOTHING LIKE a little decorator trim to transform a run-of-the-mill window treatment into an eye-catching room enhancer. A fringe, for example, can emphasize the lower edge of a valance and give it more visual separation from the fabric behind it. Gimp attached to the lower edge of a roller shade (page 47) tastefully accents its curved shape.

Trims are available in a wide range of styles and colors, many with coordinating cords, tassels, or tiebacks. They can be stitched in place, but to prevent puckering and make the application easier, even designer workrooms simply glue or fuse them. The style and thickness of the trim determine which method works best. Fusing is useful for fringes that have a relatively flat heading and when pressing won't flatten or damage the trim. Hot-gluing works better for thick headings, gimps, and cords. Fabric glue is another option, especially in small areas, but it requires extra time for drying. If desired, a continuous length of craft wire can be secured between the trim and the fabric to help curve and shape the edge.

Classic rod-pocket curtain (page 20).

HOW TO ATTACH *trims by fusing*

MATERIALS

- Decorator trim
- Liquid fray preventer
- Paper-backed fusible adhesive strips, slightly narrower than the trim or fringe heading width
- Craft wire (optional)

1. Apply liquid fray preventer liberally across the braid or fringe heading near one end; allow it to dry completely before cutting to create a clean, secure end.

2. Adjust the iron temperature to the silk setting, without steam. Working from the roll, align the paper-backed fusible adhesive strip to the back of the trim. Slide the iron along the strip at a steady pace; the iron needs only to be in contact with the fusible strip for about two seconds to create a bond. If wire is desired, feed the wire under the fusible strip as you go along. Allow the adhesive to cool.

3. Peel off the paper backing. Align the trim, adhesive side down, to the desired location on the window treatment. Allow the cut end to extend 3/4" (2 cm) beyond the finished edge of the treatment. Slide the iron along the trim at a steady pace, keeping the iron in contact with each section for six seconds or longer, depending on the thickness.

4. Stop fusing as you approach the end. Apply liquid fray preventer to the trim 3/4" (2 cm) beyond the finished edge of the treatment; allow to dry, and cut off.

5. Press again from the back side, if necessary. Wrap the ends of the trim around to the back side and fuse in place.

creative fixings

THERE ARE LOTS of beautiful choices out there for decorative rods, but they are not your only options. Sometimes the creative use of a common item finishes off the window treatment in an utterly perfect way. A casual browse through your neighborhood hardware store can give you all sorts of ideas. The key is to consider every item as a possibility and try to imagine what role it could play in a window treatment.

Tab curtain (page 24).

LEFT: Create lightweight, inexpensive poles from PVC pipe, found at the home improvement center. Clean the pipe with acetone and a soft cloth, and cut it to the correct length, using a hacksaw or PVC pipe cutter. Buy end caps to fit the pipe, and if desired, secure round ball knobs to the end caps. Mount the pipe, using wooden brackets; use keyhole brackets, such as Kirsch #5618, for center supports. Secure a short screw into the back of the pipe, with the head of the screw extending; then slide it into the keyhole slot of the bracket.

LEFT: Consider any spring-action clamping gizmo to be a potential "drapery ring." Here small plastic clamps from the hardware store couldn't be more appropriate for the theme and colors of this window topper (page 75). They suit the purpose, they look good, and they are clever as can be.

BOTTOM LEFT: Bring the outdoors inside by hanging a window treatment from a real branch. If the branch is less than 1" (2.5 cm) in diameter, mount it on rustic iron plant hangers. Mount thicker branches, using a keyhole bracket, such as Kirsch #5618. Hang a window treatment that does not require perfectly straight lines, such as tie tabs (page 29) that can be adjusted longer or shorter as needed.

BELOW: Install unusual coat hooks above the window frame to hang a triangle swag valance (page 85). Or use them to anchor tiebacks at the sides of the window.

LEFT: Looking for an ingenious way to hang a swag? Mount drawer handles vertically to the wall or upper corner of the window frame. Insert a hanger bolt into the wall or woodwork. Then attach the upper arm of the handle. Once it is screwed tightly into position, there is no need to secure the lower arm.

BELOW: Drawer knobs have all kinds of secret lives. Mounted above a window frame, knobs can offer a place for tying up slinky side panels (page 14). Secured through the slat of a roller shade, a knob offers an easy grip for raising and lowering the shade (page 49). At the ends of a simple wooden dowel, knobs become unique finials for a drapery pole or reverse roll-up shade. Replace the bolt with a hanger bolt for inserting into the wall or wood. To secure a knob through a shade slat, use a shorter bolt in the same diameter as the one that comes with the knob.

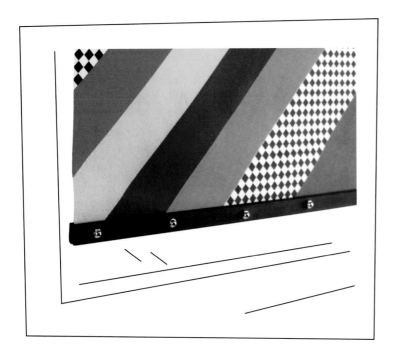

LEFT: Metal nuts, washers, and bolts add a "tech" dimension. Not merely decorative, they also secure the lower slat for this innovative roller shade (page 48) and, because of their weight, keep the shade taut and flat.

BOTTOM LEFT: Peg rail shelving above a window is not only a convenient way to hang a tab curtain (page 28), it also gives you a place to display your treasures. Peg rail mounted vertically alongside the window frame is a novel way to adjust the height of a reverse roll-up shade (page 53). If you have difficulty finding ready-to-finish peg rail, make your own from lengths of chair rail molding and shaker pegs.

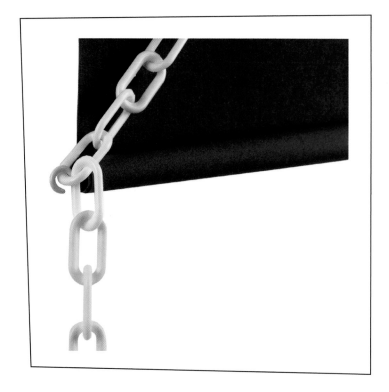

LEFT: Plastic coated utility hooks and white chain combine to make an interesting system for raising and lowering a reverse roll-up shade (page 53). Chain strung between two hooks could be used instead of a rod for hanging a one-of-a-kind curtain or top treatment.

BELOW: Use common cable ties, available at the hardware store, to hold bundled fabric for the long term. When you have a handful of folded fabric, cable ties are easier to manage than ribbon or tape ties that require two free hands. As an alternative, Velcro straps can be very useful and can be easily removed when they are no longer needed. Velcro straps are also a quick and easy way to hold back the sides of a tent flap curtain.

ABOVE: Special quilt hanging racks are useful for hanging flat window treatments like a tent flap shade (page 57). Simply mount the hanging rack and clamp the upper edge of the shade into place.

RIGHT: Grommets come in a wide range of sizes, in silver and brass colors. Look for them at fabric stores. Most manufacturers package them with installation tools and in refill packs for people who already have the tools. Follow the manufacturer's directions for installing them, and be sure to test one on a scrap of fabric folded to the same thickness as your intended target on your window treatment. Work on a hard, stable surface, such as a cement floor or a countertop, taking care to protect the surface with a piece of wood.

Use grommets to string a flat-panel curtain (page 14) onto a steel cable or thin rod. On a tent flap shade, set grommets in the upper corners for hanging the shade and in the lower corners or sides for holding the shade open (page 57).

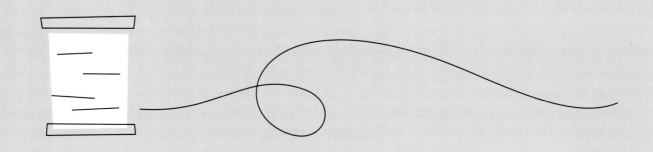

nuts and bolts

measuring and estimating yardage

THERE ARE ORDERLY steps to making any window treatment, whether it involves some sewing time or just a productive session with a glue gun:

1) Measure the window.

2) Sketch your ideas to scale.

3) Estimate the amount of fabric needed.

4) Purchase the hardware, fabric, and other supplies.

5) Measure for placement and install the hardware.

6) Remeasure from the hardware to determine the cut lengths and widths.

7) Measure and cut the fabric.

8) Make the treatment.

9) Mount the treatment.

Measuring comes into play in several of these steps, and while it seems like a no-brainer, there are some important guidelines to remember.

• Use a steel carpenter's tape measure for accuracy.

• Measure distance from the floor for the placement of hardware to ensure it will be parallel to the floor. Sometimes window frames are slightly off-square.

• Measure all the windows in a room, even if they look the same. For a uniform look, mount all the treatments at the same height, even if the windows are not.

• Allow 1/2" (1.3 cm) clearance between the bottom of a curtain and the floor when measuring for floor-length curtains. Add 2" to 4" (5 to 10 cm) of length for curtains that "brush" the floor; add 12" to 20" (30.5 to 51 cm) for curtains that puddle on the floor.

• Measure length and width of the window at three places; use the largest measurements if they vary.

The placement for rods, shade rollers, or mounting boards depends on the look you want as well as the anatomy of your window. Decorative rods are almost always mounted on the wall outside and above the window frame. The rod can extend out to the sides of the window to give the illusion of extra width or be mounted closer to the ceiling to give the illusion of extra height. Shade rollers and mounting boards can be mounted inside the window frame if they won't interfere with the operation of the window. Otherwise they are mounted at the desired height above and outside the window frame. Allow at least 2" (5 cm) of clearance between the outer treatment and any stationary or flat undertreatment, such as mini blinds, a roller shade, or pleated shade; allow 3" (7.5 cm) of clearance over traversing draperies.

For each window treatment you make, you will need to determine its finished length and width. The finished length is measured from the top of the mounting board or rod or from where you want the upper edge of a curtain to where you want the lower edge of the window treatment. The finished width is determined by measuring the length of the rod or mounting board. For treatments with returns (outer edges that wrap around a mounting board or rod ends back to the wall), the finished width includes twice the projection (distance from the wall to the front of the mounting board or rod).

Specific instructions for determining the cut lengths and widths of the fabric are given for each project in this book. In general, the cut width is determined by multiplying the finished width by the amount of fullness desired and adding the necessary allowances for side hems and any seams. Fullness describes the finished width of the curtain or valance in proportion to the length of the rod or mounting board. For example, two times fullness means that the width of the curtain measures twice the length of the rod. Yardage requirements are determined by multiplying the cut length by the number of fabric widths needed to obtain the cut width.

Window treatments made with patterned decorator fabrics usually require extra yardage in order to match the design. Add the amounts needed for any hems, rod pockets, headings, ease, and seam allowances to the finished length to determine how long the fabric lengths need to be. Then round this measurement up to the next number divisible by the size of the pattern repeat (the lengthwise distance from one distinctive point in the pattern motif to the same point in the next identical motif) to determine the cut length. For example, if the pattern repeat **(1)** is 24" (61 cm) and the needed length **(2)** is 45" (115 cm), the actual cut length **(3)** is 48" (122 cm). To have patterns match from one panel to the next, each panel must be cut at exactly the same point of the pattern repeat.

To calculate the amount of fabric needed, multiply the cut length of each piece by the number of fabric widths required for the project; add one additional pattern repeat so you can adjust the placement of the design on the cut lengths. This is the total fabric length in inches (centimeters); divide by 36" (100 cm) to determine the number of yards (meters) to buy.

Most decorator fabrics are manufactured in widths of 48" (122 cm), 54" (137 cm), or 60" (152.5 cm), with the width (selvage to selvage) intended to run horizontally. There are some fabrics, especially sheers and laces, that are manufactured up to 118" (300 cm) wide, with the width intended to run vertically (railroaded), for floor-length window treatments without vertical seams. Narrower fabrics in solid colors or nondirectional patterns can often be railroaded to avoid vertical seams in treatments such as flip toppers (page 76) or lined-to-the-edge rectangles (page 70).

MEASURING A WINDOW

LENGTH OF ROD OR
FINISHED WIDTH
OF WINDOW TREATMENT

OUTSIDE FRAME
INSIDE FRAME
LENGTH FROM ROD TO SILL
LENGTH FROM ROD TO APRON

MEASURING THE FABRIC

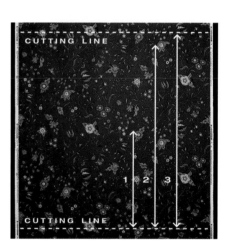

CUTTING LINE

1 2 3

CUTTING LINE

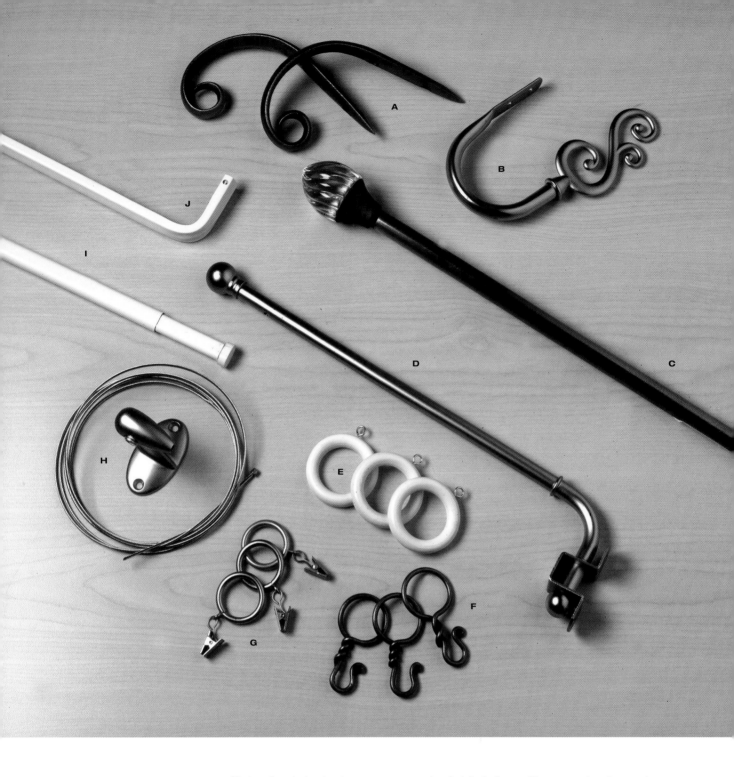

Choices for window hardware are many and varied, including multicomponent systems, where items are sold separately and can be mixed and matched to suit any purpose and style. Some items have multiple uses, such as brackets **(A)** that can also be used as holdbacks. Ornate finials can be attached to holdbacks **(B)** or poles **(C)**. Crane rods **(D)** are designed to swing away from the window. Wooden and metal rings can be slipped onto a rod and sewn **(E)** to the curtain, hooked through a buttonhole or grommet **(F)**, or clipped in place **(G)**. A steel cable system **(H)**, used instead of a rod, gives the window treatment a sleek, modern look. When the entire rod will be covered by the treatment, inexpensive utility rods, such as spring pressure rods **(I)** or oval curtain rods **(J)** can be used.

selecting and installing hardware

WINDOW TREATMENT HARDWARE is available in a wide range of styles to suit any decorating plan. Some rods, such as utility curtain rods and spring pressure rods, are designed to be covered completely by the fabric. Others may have decorative finishes, ornate finials, and stylish rings that enhance the treatment. Decorative swag holders, tieback holders, and curtain holdbacks add designer touches to even the simplest treatments. Lots of alternative items can also be used for mounting various treatment styles (pages 118 to 123). It is important to select and install the hardware before measuring for the cut length and width of the treatment.

Window treatment hardware is usually packaged complete with mounting brackets, screws or nails, and installation instructions. Additional center support brackets may be needed for exceptionally wide or heavy treatments. Some companies sell interchangeable parts in separate packages, such as rods that coordinate with several different finial and ring styles or poles and brackets that are sold separately.

The instructions that accompany the hardware don't necessarily tell you everything you need to know, so here are a few professional tips and techniques to fill in the information gaps.

• Use screws alone if you are installing through drywall or plaster directly into wall studs. You may not know whether or not you are installing into a stud until you have drilled your first hole. If the screws supplied are not long enough to go at least 1" (2.5 cm) into the stud, replace them with longer screws of the same size.

• When the brackets are not positioned over studs, support the screws for lightweight treatments with plastic sleeve anchors (page 131) in the correct size for the screws.

• If the brackets must support a heavy treatment, use plastic toggle anchors (page 130) in the correct size for your wallboard depth, or use molly bolts (page 131).

• If nails are supplied with the hardware you purchased, use them only for lightweight treatments installed directly to the window frame. Otherwise, substitute screws or molly bolts that fit through the holes in the brackets.

• Sleeve anchors, toggle anchors, and molly bolts are not usually supplied with the hardware.

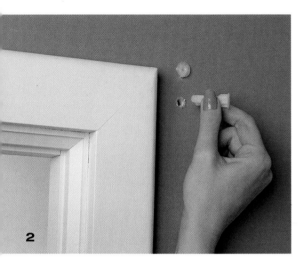

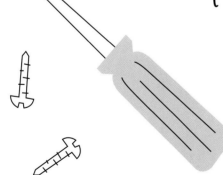

plastic toggle anchors

1. Mark the screw locations on the wall. Drill holes for the plastic toggle anchors, using a bit slightly smaller than the diameter of the toggle anchor shaft.

2. Squeeze the wings of the toggle flat, and push the anchor into the hole; tap in place with a hammer until it is flush with the wall.

3. Insert the screw through the bracket hole and into the installed anchor; tighten the screw. The wings spread out and flatten against the back side of the drywall.

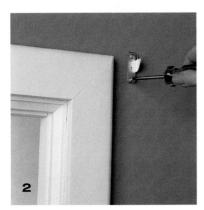

plastic sleeve anchors

1. Mark screw locations on the wall. Drill holes for the plastic anchors, using a drill bit slightly smaller than the diameter of the anchor. Tap anchors into holes, using a hammer.

2. Insert the screw through the bracket hole and into the installed anchor. Tighten the screw securely; the anchor expands in the drywall, preventing it from pulling out.

HOW TO INSTALL BRACKETS USING molly bolts

1. Mark the bolt locations on the wall. Drill holes for molly bolts, using a bit slightly small than the diameter of the molly bolt casing.

2. Tap the molly bolt casing into the drilled hole, using a hammer; insert and tighten the bolt. The molly bolt casing expands and flattens against the back side of the drywall.

3. Remove the bolt from the casing; insert the bolt through the bracket hole and into the installed casing. Screw the bracket securely in place.

covering and installing mounting boards

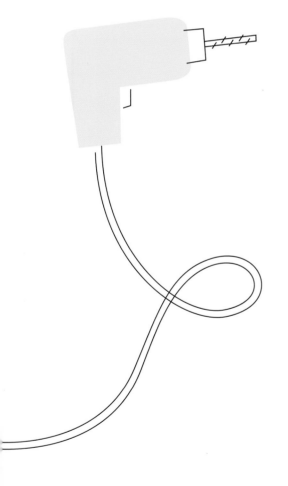

WINDOW TREATMENTS such as tent flap shades, Roman shades, and many toppers are mounted on boards instead of drapery hardware. The treatment can be installed as an outside mount or an inside mount, depending on the look preferred and the depth of the window frame. For an outside mount, the treatment is installed on the wall above and just to the outside of the frame. For an inside mount, the window frame must be deep enough to accommodate a 1×2 board, allowing the treatment to be flush with the front of the frame, without hampering the operation of the window.

Use pine lumber in 1×2 size for inside mounts or in 1×4 or 1×6 sizes for outside mounts, choosing wider boards for toppers that must allow room for undertreatments. Cut outside-mount board to the finished width of the treatment. Cut inside-mount boards 1/2" (1.3 cm) shorter than the desired finished width. If the ends of the mounting board are likely to show from the side (for example, on an outside mounted Roman shade), cover the board with fabric to match the window treatment.

HOW TO COVER A *mounting board*

1. Cut fabric to cover the board with the width equal to the board circumference plus 1" (2.5 cm) and the length equal to the board length plus 3" (7.5 cm).

2. Center the board on the wrong side of the fabric. Staple one long edge to the board, placing staples about 8" (20.5 cm) apart, stopping within 6" (15 cm) of the ends. Fold under the remaining long edge, wrap it over the board, and staple in place, again leaving the ends free.

3. Wrap the fabric over the ends, mitering out the fullness. Staple in place.

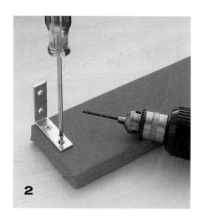  

HOW TO INSTALL AN *outside-mounted board*

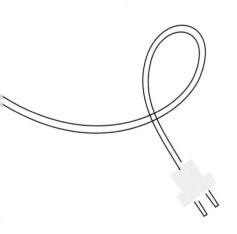

1. Select angle irons that are more than one-half the board width. Align the angle irons to the bottom, back edge and mark the screw holes, positioning them within 1" (2.5 cm) of the ends and at 45" (115 cm) intervals or less.

2. Predrill screw holes into the board, using a bit slightly smaller than the screws. Screw the angle irons to the board.

3. Hold the board at the desired placement, making sure it is level; mark the screw holes on the wall. Remove the angle irons from the board.

4. Secure the angle irons to the wall, using 1¹/₂" (3.8 cm) flat-head screws into wall studs. If the angle irons are not positioned at wall studs, use molly bolts, sleeve anchors, or toggle anchors (pages 130 to 131).

5. Attach the window treatment to the mounting board. Place the board on the angle irons, aligning the screw holes, and fasten the screws.

HOW TO INSTALL AN
inside-mounted board

1. Position the board flush with the front of the frame. From the bottom of the board, predrill screw holes through the board and up into the window frame, 2" (5 cm) from the ends and again in the center, if necessary.

2. Attach the window treatment to the board. Poke holes through the fabric at the locations of the screw holes, using an awl. Align the predrilled holes, and secure the treatment to the frame, using size 8 × 1¹/2" (3.8 cm) pan-head screws.

HOW TO INSTALL A roman
shade with
minimal projection

Install the board flat to the wall at the desired location above the window, predrilling holes through the board into the wall. Secure with size 8 × 2¹/2" (6.5 cm) flat-head screws into wall studs. Or use molly bolts, sleeve anchors, or toggle anchors (page 130) if not screwing into wall studs.

preparing and cutting fabric

EVEN QUICK AND easy window treatments have a more professional look when extra care is taken in the preparation and cutting of the fabric. While decorator fabrics are not your only option, keep in mind that they are manufactured to be more stable and durable than fashion fabrics and often have added finishes to make them more fade-resistant, water repellent, or stain-resistant. Printed or patterned decorator fabrics, unlike fashion fabrics, are printed so that the pattern repeats vertically at regular intervals. If your treatment requires two or more widths of fabric to be stitched together, the pattern can be matched up at the seams, thus disguising the seamline.

Preshrinking is recommended to ensure that fabrics will not shrink during construction or when the treatment is first cleaned. If the fabric is washable, launder the uncut piece at the same water and dryer temperatures you intend to use for the finished treatment. If the fabric is not washable, preshrink it with a steam iron.

Window treatments are only washable if they are made with washable, preshrunk fabric and have no other nonwashable components, such as lining or decorative trims. Window treatments that are not washable should be dry-cleaned when necessary. Occasional vacuuming is sufficient for many styles.

MATCHING PATTERNED FABRIC

SEAM HERE TO CONTINUE PATTERN

PATTERN REPEAT

SELVAGE

CROSSWISE GRAIN
=54" (137 CM)

ABOVE: Mark tightly woven unpatterned fabrics perpendicular to the selvages, using a carpenter's square. Cut along the marked lines.

BELOW: For lightweight or loosely woven fabrics, pull out a yarn along the crosswise grain, from selvage to selvage. Cut along the line left by the missing yarn.

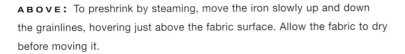

ABOVE: To preshrink by steaming, move the iron slowly up and down the grainlines, hovering just above the fabric surface. Allow the fabric to dry before moving it.

To ensure that the treatment will hang straight, the fabric lengths must be cut on-grain, perpendicular to the selvages. Patterned decorator fabrics are cut following the pattern repeat, so it is important to check that they are printed on grain before buying the fabric. To cut printed decorator fabric, mark both selvages at the exact same point in the pattern repeat. Using a long straightedge, draw a line connecting the two points. Cut on the marked line.

sewing seams and hems

EVEN IF YOU are not an accomplished sewer, window treatments, especially the ones in this book, are easily within your reach. Any seams that need to be sewn are done in straight lines with a simple straight stitch. The techniques described here result in secure seams that can withstand daily opening and closing and occasional cleaning. They are the same steps that would be followed in a professional drapery workroom, but you can cut some corners if you want to. For instance, if the seams are in stationary curtain panels that aren't constantly in contact with a moveable undertreatment and will never be laundered, what will cause them to fray? You could opt to leave the seam allowances unfinished. And, if leaving the selvages intact doesn't make the seams pucker, where's the harm?

There is one technique that must be followed if you don't want your curtains to scream "made by an amateur!" Patterned decorator fabrics should always be matched at the seams, and the pattern should fall in the same place on separate curtain panels. In fact, if you are making curtains for more than one window in the same room, you should be able to follow the pattern around the room at the same level. So all of your cut lengths are made at the same point in the pattern.

Hems can be made in several ways. Ideally, the raw edge is encased in a double-fold hem, stitched in place with a straight stitch or a machine- or hand-sewn blind hem. Hems in mediumweight fabric can also be fused in place, using narrow strips of paper-backed fusible adhesive. Keep in mind that most fusible adhesives will not hold up through dry-cleaning. The depth of the hem varies with its position—whether it is at the side or bottom of the treatment—and, for bottom hems, the length of the style, as detailed in the charts on pages 13 and 18.

HOW TO MATCH *seams in a patterned fabric*

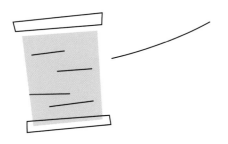

1. Place the two fabric widths right sides together, aligning the selvages. Fold back the upper selvage until the pattern matches up exactly. Press the foldline.

2. Unfold the pressed edge, and pin the fabrics together in the foldline.

3. Turn the fabric over, and check the match from the right side. Make any necessary adjustments.

CONTINUED

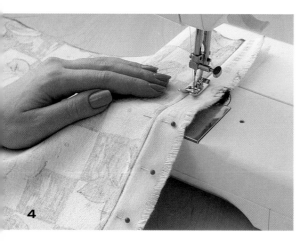

4. Repin the fabric so the pins are perpendicular to the foldline. Stitch the seam directly into the fold.

5. Check the match from the right side again. Make any necessary adjustments. Trim away the selvages to within 1/2" (1.3 cm) of the seam. Finish the seam allowances together and press them to one side. Or clip into the selvages every 2" (5 cm) at a slight diagonal to within 1/8" (3 mm) of the stitching, to allow the seam to relax.

6. Repeat steps 1 to 5 for all additional fabric widths in the same curtain panel. Trim the entire panel to the necessary cut length. (Remember you initially cut the fabric extra long to allow you to match the pattern.)

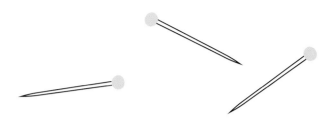

HOW TO STITCH A *double-fold hem*

1. Place the fabric face-down on a pressing surface. Turn under the entire amount allowed for the hem, such as 8" (20.5 cm) for a bottom hem on long curtains. Press the fold.

2. Unfold the pressed edge. Turn the raw edge under, aligning it to the pressed foldline. Press the fold.

3. Refold the hem along the pressed foldlines, encasing the raw edge to form a double-fold hem. Pin the hem in place and stitch along the inner fold.

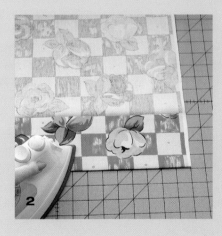

index